Fasting
Made
Easy

DON COLBERT, MD

SILOAM
A STRANG COMPANY

Most Strang Communications/Charisma House/Siloam products are available at special quantity discounts for bulk purchase for sales promotions, premiums, fund-raising, and educational needs. For details, write Strang Communications/Charisma House/Siloam, 600 Rinehart Road, Lake Mary, Florida 32746, or telephone (407) 333-0600.

Fasting Made Easy by Don Colbert, MD
Published by Siloam
A Strang Company
600 Rinehart Road
Lake Mary, Florida 32746
www.siloam.com

Unless otherwise noted, all Scripture quotations are from the New American Standard Bible. Copyright © 1960, 1962, 1963, 1968, 1971, 1972, 1973, 1975, 1977 by the Lockman Foundation. Used by permission. (www.Lockman.org)

Scripture quotations marked KJV are from the King James Version of the Bible.

Scripture quotations marked NKJV are from the New King James Version of the Bible. Copyright © 1979, 1980, 1982 by Thomas Nelson, Inc., publishers. Used by permission.

Cover design by Judith McKittrick
Interior design by Terry Clifton

Library of Congress Cataloging-in-Publication Data
Colbert, Don.
  Fasting made easy / Don Colbert.
    p. cm.
  Includes bibliographical references.
  ISBN 1-59185-451-2 (casebound)
  1. Fasting. 2. Fasting--Health aspects. 3. Detoxification
(Health)
  I. Title.
  RM226.C65 2004
  613.2--dc22

                                        2004006320

05 06 07 08 — 9876543
Printed in the United States of America

Contents

Introduction

What—me, fast? Forget it!

Most of us, if we think about fasting at all, think of it as something we would never voluntarily do. Oh, we might do it once in a blue moon—on doctor's orders or if we're seeking God for an especially important decision. But it's certainly not something we would ever consider making part of our lifestyle. Life is uncertain enough as it is without *intentionally* skipping meals!

And yet you have picked up this book. Something in you is drawn to the idea of fasting. Maybe you have heard what a great method it is to detoxify your body. Or maybe you are wanting to step up your walk with Christ and make fasting a spiritual discipline you can embrace. Maybe a little of both.

Either way, *Fasting Made Easy* is for you.

Fasting is good for you on so many levels. There are few things you can do for your body that have the power to so radically improve your physical health that fasting has. We live in a toxic environment, and fasting is a mighty cleanser. On the spiritual side, fasting begins to break the stranglehold your hunger may have over your behavior. The Bible talks about this as the flesh warring against the spirit. Fasting is part of crucifying the flesh, which leads to greater self-control and harmony with God's Spirit.

There are a number of different kinds of fasts. Some are more radical than others. Some restrict food and drink exclusively, while others ask you to abstain from something else—like watching television, perhaps. The kind of fasting I recommend in this book, juice fasting, is extremely helpful to clean out the toxins in your body and may help jump-start you into a healthy lifestyle that includes periodic fasting. I hope it will bring you closer to God as well.

So don't be alarmed. Fasting doesn't have to be scary. It will improve your health physically and spiritually. And I will be with you every step of the way.

Chapter 1

WHY SHOULD I FAST?

If you have watched a news telecast in the last year, you have listened to reports of the perils of the polluted environment in which we live. Environmentalists continually plead for help to save our world from air pollution and water pollution as well as from other "causes" that involve preserving and restoring our good green earth.

Unfortunately, in spite of their pleas, the world you live in is increasingly more dangerous to your health with every passing day. The air you breathe is filled with industrial air pollution, along with carbon monoxide and other elements that threaten your health. In addition, the unrestrained use of chemicals in many businesses is contaminating your environment and damaging your health. Common household cleaners and other personal products contaminate your home environment as well.

Threat of a Toxic Environment

You can live without food for several weeks and without water for several days, but you can only live for minutes without air. However, breathing polluted air can be detrimental to your health. When the air you breathe is polluted, dangerous contaminants pour into your lungs and through your bloodstream, and they are eventually pumped by your heart to every cell in your body. Even air-conditioned buildings, where many people spend the majority of their time, are not free from harmful toxins, chemicals, and bacteria that get trapped in the building and are recirculated through heating and air-conditioning systems.

Sick building syndrome

Out-gassing is a term used to describe the air contamination of new buildings, where building materials emit harmful gasses—such as formaldehyde from carpets, solvents from paints, and other chemicals from fabrics, couches, curtains, glues, and more—into the air. Older buildings may emit airborne mold, dust mites, or dangerous bacteria, which are pumped into the air through air-conditioning units. Volatile organic compounds are also emitted from copying machines, laser printers, computers, and other office equipment.

How does the pollution of "inside" air affect your body? Referred to as "sick building syndrome," many ailments can be directly related to these unhealthy breathing conditions. If the building where you work does not have clean air, you may experience headaches;

itchy, red, and watery eyes; sore throat; dizziness; nausea—as well as problems concentrating. Other symptoms of sick building syndrome include fatigue, shortness of breath, and problems with memory.

This information regarding environmental hazards is not meant to make you feel helpless but to help answer the question, "Why should I fast?" Considering the impact of a toxic environment on your body, you will be relieved to know that fasting can cleanse your body and help you overcome the health threats of a toxic environment.

Symptoms from pesticide pollution

Outside air is hardly exempt from pollutants. Pesticides are not only used in fields of crops and on trees and flowers, but they can also be found in air fresheners, mattresses, disposable diapers, carpets, and many other products. Your skin readily absorbs pesticides, which are also breathed into your lungs and can be ingested by your mouth. Your body is designed to eliminate these dangerous poisons, but the sheer quantity to which you are exposed daily can overwhelm your body's defense systems.

When pesticides build up to a dangerous level in your body, you may actually begin to experience memory loss, depression, anxiety, psychosis, or other forms of mental illness. Parkinson's disease and possibly even hormone-sensitive cancers, such as breast and prostate cancer, can be related to this toxic buildup. Many people who suffer with neurological diseases sometimes have higher levels of pesticides stored in their brains.

Pesticides in the body are stored in fatty tissues. You need to consider those "love handles" a hiding place for stored toxins and poisons. Your brain, which is composed of about 60 percent lipids (fat-like substances), will also readily store these poisons. Other fatty tissues that store toxins include the breasts and prostate gland.

A danger of very-low-calorie diets is that they allow these toxins from stored fat to be released so quickly that you may feel foggy-minded and fatigued. Your liver, which is one of the main cleansing organs of your body, can become overwhelmed and unable to break down and eliminate the quantity of toxins released by your body during dieting. When that happens, even more toxins may become stored in the brain and other fatty tissues.

In contrast, fasting, when done correctly, can help to rid the body of this toxic overload and restore health and vitality to your body, mind, and spirit.

Problems from other contaminants

While we cannot discuss at length all the potential contaminants that overload your body with toxins, I want to mention a few of the most common and most hazardous to your health. Cigarette smoke, which contains cadmium, cyanide, lead, arsenic, tars, radio-active material, and other deadly poisons, overloads your body with these toxins. And the negative effects of inhaling "secondhand smoke" are well documented. That is why I do not recommend "smoking sections" in restaurants. It makes about as much sense as having a "peeing section" in a swimming pool.

It is important to mention the toxins in your water, many of which come from chemicals emitted into our air and washed down into our water supplies by rain. For example, the Kellogg Report showed that the growth of industry in this country has introduced complex and sometimes lethal pollutants into our nation's water systems.[1] Chlorine, which is added to the water to kill microorganisms, can combine with organic materials to form trihalomethanes, which are cancer-promoting substances. Although chlorine kills most bacteria, it does not kill viruses and parasites, such as *Giardia*, one of the major causes of diarrhea in day-care centers.

Another major problem is solvents, such as those used in cleaning products, which dissolve other ma-terials that otherwise would not be soluble in water. These can be very damaging to your kidneys and liver. Like pesticides, they are likely to be stored in your fatty tissues, including the breasts, prostate, and brain. There are more than 60,000 chemicals already in our environment, with about 2,000 more being added each year.[2]

Even your food may be filled with a long list of chemical substances added for flavor, color, or longer shelf life. Chemical food additives are usually made from petroleum or coal tar products. They may include preservatives, bleaching agents, emulsifiers, texturizers, and ripening agents (such as ethylene gas) sprayed on bananas and other fruits. In short, much of the food we consume adds to the toxicity of the body, as we will discuss.

A TESTIMONY

(Adapted from Jeff Louderback, "Delivered From Pain," *Charisma and Christian Life*, November 2003, 46.)

When he awakens in the morning, Russ Stewart celebrates the simple acts of taking a shower, dressing himself, and taking a walk before beginning the day. To him, there is no reason to dread Mondays—or any day. The thirty-eight-year-old pastor is now free from debilitating medical conditions that had plagued him with anguishing pain from the time he was a child in Oklahoma until he was introduced to Don Colbert's body-detoxification program last April.

A doctor had diagnosed the eleven-year-old Stewart with juvenile arthritis, which caused swollen joints and impaired his mobility. Stewart was unable to participate in physical activities—no baseball at the neighborhood park or basketball on the playground. And it was only the beginning of the "sometimes tortuous" pain that gradually worsened as he grew from a boy into a man.

In his early twenties, doctors discovered that Stewart had psoriasis and psoriatic arthritis. As the years passed, his fingers and toes became crooked. His knees and hips chronically ached. He was prescribed so many medications—everything from anti-inflammatories to methotrexate, a drug that was originally used to treat cancer—that a briefcase was needed to carry them all.

The heavy doses of medicine left his immune system weak, and he was prone to viruses such as colds and the flu. Typically, he took as many as eight 600-milligram ibuprofen tablets to make it through the day. "I was constantly worried about losing my job," says Stewart, who was an administrator at an assisted-living facility before becoming senior adult ministries director at Elsinore First Assembly in Lake Elsinore, California. By then, Stewart was also suffering from fibromyalgia and migraine headaches that caused him to miss work due to their severity. "I was so disabled with the arthritis that my wife had to put my shoes and socks on because I couldn't bend down," says Stewart. "At church, I wanted to lift my hands in worship, but I couldn't."

Stewart became so discouraged from the constant pain that he felt he couldn't go on. He believes that God intervened for him, hearing his desperate prayers and sparking his dramatic recovery. While surfing the TV channels during the early hours of the morning one sleepless night, he found the Richard Roberts' Christian talk show on which Dr. Don Colbert was a guest. He was talking about his book *Toxic Relief.*

Stewart ordered the book, read it, and followed Dr. Colbert's comprehensive dietary guidelines. After finishing a three-week, three-day detoxification program, Stewart began to notice dramatic improvements in his health. Within five weeks of beginning the program, Stewart's skin was smooth and clear, his migraine headaches never returned, and his joints were free of pain. He could walk without discomfort, and he began to play golf for the first time. "I had been so sick for so long, it was like waking up from a coma," Stewart explained.

"When my mother saw me for the first time after I was well, she cried. She had not seen me well since I was a little boy." Stewart's mother also followed Dr. Colbert's detoxification program and is now pain-free and off all medications for osteoarthritis from which she suffered.

Give Your Body a Boost

I don't mean for the discussion regarding our polluted environment to make you feel like a victim or to cause you to give in to hopelessness. On the contrary; as I have mentioned, I only want to highlight the problem of our toxic environment in answer to the question, *"Why should I fast?"* As we discuss the effectiveness of fasting to cleanse the body of tremendous amounts of toxins, it will become clearer to you why you need to include fasting as part of your lifestyle for health.

Of course, there are other ways, along with fasting, to help you in your fight against this inevitable toxic overload. The following section will be helpful in your quest to give your body a boost by learning to avoid major sources of pollutants.

How to Avoid Major Sources of Pollutants

- Avoid heavy smog and gasoline fumes. Wait inside at an airport away from exhaust and fumes from buses and taxis; never jog alongside a busy highway.
- Choose less toxic carpets, paints, and drapes; never use furniture made of pressed wood or particleboard.
- Minimize your exposure to mold spores and dust mites by keeping the air-conditioning and heating ducts in your home clean, changing the filters regularly. Lowering the relative humidity in your home to less than 45 percent will discourage the growth of mold and dust mites.

- Use an air purifier such as a hepa filter or ionizer air filter in your home to remove chemicals and toxins in the air. Get fresh air from the outdoors into your home during the day.
- Reduce your exposure to pesticides by not having your home sprayed. Try natural methods of bug control, such as sprinkling closets with boric acid.
- Avoid use of air fresheners or air deodorizers.
- Removing shoes before coming inside from outdoors will eliminate a major source of pesticides.
- Don't allow smoking in your home, and avoid areas where secondhand smoke is present.
- Use a water filter for drinking water and a shower filter, such as a Wellness Filter, charcoal, or KDF shower filter, to effectively remove chlorine.[3] (See Appendix D.)

While these are helpful ways to avoid some of the mentioned contaminants, it is impossible to keep the body from being exposed to toxins. Fasting is an effective means of cleansing the body of these undesirable toxins, which, if left unchecked, can cause your health to deteriorate in a number of ways.

The Threat From Internal Toxins

Before discussing how effective fasting can be for restoring and maintaining health, let me address briefly another reason to include periodic fasting as a part of your healthy lifestyle—*internal toxins*. I like to compare the wonderful complexities of your body to a fine engine of an expensive automobile. Just like that engine, which creates exhaust as it burns fuel to run, your body creates many different toxins as it burns the "fuel" you feed it. Your body is equipped to eliminate these toxins through special functions of the liver, the GI tract, and other body systems to keep you feeling energetic and healthy. The problem arises when these built-in elimination systems are bombarded both from without and within with more toxins than they were designed to handle.

The downside of antibiotics

You may be aware that your intestines should contain adequate amounts of good bacteria, such as *lactobacillus acidophilus* and *bifidus*, which are designed to prevent the growth of bad bacteria and yeast. In the event that you develop sinusitis, bronchitis, tonsillitis, or other common "reasons" for taking antibiotics, the attempt of the antibiotics to kill the bad bacteria results in their eliminating many of the good bacteria as well. When excessive amounts of beneficial bacteria are killed, pathogenic bacteria may flourish. The bad bacteria may actually produce *endotoxins* internally, which may be as toxic as almost any chemical, pesticide, or solvent that enters your body from outside sources. Though antibiotics are important in treating life-threatening infections, the negative effects on health from *overuse* of antibiotics are beginning to be evaluated seriously by the medical community.

The effect of antibiotics upsetting the body's delicate balance of good bacteria can result in yeast overgrowth, called *candidiasis*, with an array of unpleasant symptoms, including bloating, gas, and irritable bowel syndrome. Candidiasis is caused by overgrowth of yeast in the intestines and may release over eighty different toxins into the body, including acetaldehyde and ethanol, which is alcohol. Acetaldehyde is related to formaldehyde, which is found in carpets and pressed wood. Acetaldehyde is extremely toxic to the brain, causing memory loss, depression, severe fatigue, and difficulty with concentration.

The problem of free radicals
The body also suffers from the internal production of *free radicals*, a result of the oxidation process of foods. For example, when you cut an apple in half and leave it in the air, it turns brown—that is oxidation. In the process of converting foods to energy (ATP), some free radicals are always produced. However, certain foods such as fried foods and polyunsaturated fats, including most salad dressings, cause production of excessive amounts of dangerous free

radicals. Though your body's trillions of cells have a protective wrapping around them made of lipids or "fatty" cell membranes, excessive amounts of free radicals released into your tissues can work like wrecking balls, ricocheting off the protective cell membranes and damaging them in the process.

Imagine what would happen to the city of New York if a large crane were driven through its streets with a giant, uncontrolled wrecking ball swinging from side to side. Even if it did not actually bring down the skyscrapers, it could inflict severe damage to them. Similarly, free radicals released into your tissues can wreak havoc on your internal organs as well.

Victims of the "American" Diet

In addition to the threat of internal toxins, the standard American diet (SAD) presents another challenge to your health. We have become a nation of sugar addicts. "Added sugars, found largely in junk foods such as soft drinks, cakes, and cookies, squeeze healthier foods out of the diet. Sugar now accounts for 16 percent of the calories consumed by the average American and 20 percent of teenagers' calories."[4] A USDA survey shows that the average American is consuming about 20 teaspoons of sugar per day.[5] That results in over 150 pounds of sugar consumed a year per person, largely through sodas, which contain 9 teaspoons per 12-ounce can.[6]

Sugar woes

People continue to believe that a little sugar will not hurt them. However, continuing to eat this "dead food" on a scale that the average American consumes it can cause serious health problems. Everyone knows that sugar is linked to diabetes; it is also associated with hypoglycemia—low blood sugar. That is because if excessive amounts of sugar are eaten, the body produces excessive amounts of insulin to handle the sugar overload, which may drive the blood sugar too low, resulting in hypoglycemia.

Sugar is also a major cause of obesity, a weakened immune system, behavioral disorders, osteoporosis, yeast overgrowth (candidiasis), accelerated aging, and sugar addictions. These cravings for more, caused by consumption of sugar, may lead to binge eating. You plan to eat only one cookie, but one leads to another, and you continue eating until the entire box of cookies has been devoured. And, of course, these episodes of binge eating can lead to more serious eating disorders.

Worthless white flour

Another dead food that is a "staple" of the average American diet is white flour. White flour is created by removing the outer fibrous portion from the whole grain. That shell contains healthy fiber and B vitamins. Then, the germ of the wheat is also extracted, which contains the majority of the nutrients—vitamin E, the B vitamins, and minerals. After extracting these "live" parts of the grain, the starch, or *endosperm*, remains, which is then ground into white flour with practically zero nutritional value. Consider this: the live parts of the grain are then marketed to health food stores as wheat germ and fiber—go figure.

Meat worries

One of the reasons Americans rank high in heart disease and cancer is that we also score high in our consumption of red meat. People who choose to live on hamburgers, steaks, pork chops, and ham sand-wiches are going to suffer the consequences in poor health. Consuming excess meat and protein (including milk products, cheeses, and eggs) congests the organs and cells. It lowers the pH of the tissues, making the cells constipated from protein overload. When that happens, the cells become acidic and may not be able to adequately release their waste products. The benefit of fasting simply cannot be overestimated to help the body rid itself of these accumulated toxins.

Salt wiles

The typical American consumes excessive amounts of salt. Most of our food is processed, which usually means it is full of salt, because salt is a preservative that prolongs the shelf life of food products. The wiles of salt working inside our bodies may lead to high blood pressure along with other health problems. I see patients every day with blood pressure problems. For some, medication is needed at least temporarily to correct this dangerous condition. Others, simply by making a few healthy lifestyle choices, including limiting salt intake and practicing periodic fasting, can greatly improve their blood pressure.

These and many other unnecessary health conditions can be improved and eliminated by choosing to give your toxic body welcome relief through periodic fasting.

Enhancing the Design

Let me rush to the good news at this point: your body is designed with an incredible system of defense, which can be enhanced and, in some cases, restored, through proper fasting. Even though your body is bombarded by external and internal toxins, you can choose to step in and even the score.

The burden of toxins your body is fighting has been accumulating over time. You may have become accustomed to the general feeling of fatigue and general lack of vitality that toxicity causes. You may even be suffering from symptoms of a degenerative disease. If so, you will be amazed at how much better you will feel after choosing to cleanse your body through fasting.

In my experience as a physician, I have seen heart disease, diabetes, hypertension, arthritis, chronic fatigue, and many other serious diseases reversed as my patients cleanse their bodies from toxins through fasting. In addition, detoxifying your body through fasting can also help to rid you of excess weight, if you are overweight or even obese. Not only will you feel better and live longer as you remove toxins from your body, but you will look better as well. Eyes become brighter and skin glows as you enjoy the vitality of higher energy levels.

I trust I have been able to answer the question, *"Why should I fast?"* As you continue to read, you will discover other benefits as well for choosing to work with your body's designed ability to cleanse and heal itself. Though fasting may seem like a "sacrifice" at first, I want you to understand the wonderful potential it has for enhancing your health and helping you to maintain a healthy lifestyle.

Chapter 2

PHYSICAL BENEFITS OF FASTING

As we continue to explore the need for fasting, we will consider the many benefits it provides to our bodies, minds, and spirits. Medical science is recognizing more and more the innate connection between these inseparable facets of our being. What we eat affects our moods and, to a certain extent, even our attitudes. What we think affects how our bodies digest food; it also impacts the way we handle stress. And our spiritual well-being is influenced by our physical and mental health. A simple example of these interrelated processes is the well-documented example of hyperactivity in children triggered by food additives and colorings such as red dye. Other "foods" that are well documented for their negative effect on our minds and emotions are sugar and caffeine.

Fasting: A Rest From Food

Periodic rest from food, known as *fasting*, provides fantastic health benefits to your body, mind, and spirit. For example, fasting gives a restorative rest to your digestive tract. Every day your body spends a great amount of energy in digesting, absorbing, and assimilating food.

Periodic fasting gives your digestive tract a chance to rest and repair. The body's designed healing processes automatically work when given a chance to rest from other activities. This rest from "digestion as usual" in turn allows your overburdened liver to catch up with its task of detoxification.

Your blood and your lymphatic system also receive needed cleansing of toxic buildup through fasting as well. During fasting, your cells, tissues, and organs dump out accumulated waste products from cellular metabolism, as well as harmful chemicals and other toxins. And your other digestive organs, including the stomach, pancreas, intestines, and gallbladder, get a much deserved rest during fasting, which allows your cells time to heal, repair, and be strengthened.

A powerful, natural way to bring relief to your body from the burden of excess toxicity, fasting is also a safe way to heal the body from degenerative disease. The primary way that fasting allows your body to heal is by giving it a rest. As with all living things, you need to rest. Sleeping is not the only kind of rest you need. Your digestive system and other organs need a rest from their work as well.

Biblical principle of rest

This understanding of the human's need for rest is not new to mankind. God introduced the principle of a "Sabbath rest" to His ancient Jewish nation. It is one of the Ten Commandments of the law of God: "Remember the sabbath day, to keep it holy" (Exod. 20:8). Israel was given specific instructions regarding this divine command to work six days and to rest on the seventh day of each week. This principle of rest was important as well to their agricultural system. The Israelites were commanded to allow their fields to lie fallow every seventh year in order to give the soil the "rest" it needed to reestablish its own mineral and nutrient content. (See Leviticus 25:1–7.)

Because this biblical agricultural principle of resting the soil has been ignored by virtually all modern farmers, the soil has become depleted of some of the minerals and other nutrients that our bodies crave for health. And chemical fertilizers do not succeed in giving us the abundant mineral content of healthy soil. Because we do not get the nutrition we need from our food, the result is often eating more to try to satisfy the body's craving for nourishment. This, in part, is the cause of rampant obesity, resulting from being overfed and undernourished.

Wisdom of the animal kingdom

It is interesting to note that in the animal kingdom, it is a natural habit to seek rest and to abstain from food, especially when the animal is sick or injured.

A sick animal refuses to eat and finds a place to rest where it can lap up water and be safe. Some animals hibernate, resting for an entire season without eating.

Rest is also a powerful principle of healing for the human body and psyche. Every night as you sleep, you are providing refreshing rest for your mind and body, which aids health in a tremendous way. Sleep deprivation is a commonly known form of torture, emphasizing the fact of our innate need for rest.

Fasting may be considered an "internal" rest for the body, allowing it to restore vitality and energy to vital organs by activating the marvelous self-cleansing system with which it is designed.

Enjoying the Physical Benefits of Fasting

To help convince you of the potentially healing benefits of fasting, let me explain briefly the marvelous natural detoxification system God designed for your body. Proper understanding of the innate healing power resident in your body will help you appreciate the phenomenal benefits of fasting.

Protect your natural detox system.

The hardest working organ in the body is the liver. Weighing about five pounds, it is also the largest single organ in the body, about the size of a football. It is designed to perform about five hundred functions for the health of the body. The five main functions are:

1. Filtering your blood to remove toxins such as viruses, bacteria, and yeast
2. Storing vitamins, minerals, and carbohydrates
3. Processing fats, proteins, and carbohydrates
4. Producing bile to break down fats for digestion
5. Breaking down and detoxifying the body of hormones, chemicals, toxins, and metabolic waste

It only takes one minute for your liver to filter about two quarts of the five quarts of blood your body contains. To appreciate the magnitude of this feat, you could compare your liver to the filter in a swimming pool. The filter would need to clean half of the pool's water every minute to keep up with what your liver can do. What an incredibly powerful filter your liver is! If it is working efficiently, it can filter out 99 percent of the bacteria and other toxins in your blood before sending the cleansed blood back into circulation.

You also need to understand the important detoxification task your liver does by removing toxins in the "bile." Every day your liver produces about a quart of bile, which helps to digest dietary fats, breaking them down into a form that can be used as fuel for the body. The bile also functions to eliminate poisonous toxins from your body, flushing them out through your colon. For a more complete discussion of these important detoxifying functions of your liver, please read my book *Toxic Relief.*

Unfortunately, when this natural filter gets overwhelmed with toxins, it cannot function well, much as a dirty air filter in your car cannot remove dirt from the air. Your liver may get overloaded with toxins from our food and water, from food allergies, parasites, toxins in the air, toxins in the home or workplace, and from free radicals produced internally in the liver by the detoxification process itself. Like dust and dirt that accumulate in your air filter, these toxins make the liver work too hard; eventually, it cannot function efficiently. That is why fasting becomes important, to allow the liver to rest and be able to catch up with its cleansing duties.

Some signs of liver toxicity include the following:

- Pallid skin
- A coated tongue
- Bad breath
- Skin rashes
- Poor skin tone
- Itchy, weepy, swollen, and red eyes
- Yellow discoloration of the eyes
- Offensive body odor
- Itchy skin
- Altered or bitter taste in your mouth

Because the liver is such an important organ for detoxifying the body, it is vital that you have a healthy liver in order to be healthy on this toxic planet. You must keep this champion prizefighter healthy and working at peak efficiency. Fasting is a wonderful way to improve the efficiency of your detoxification system. However, before you begin your fast, it is important that you follow a two-week nutritional program (four weeks if you are extremely toxic) designed to support and strengthen your liver. (See Appendix A for detailed instructions.)

Restore a healthy GI tract.

Have you ever worked on a computer that was overloaded with files, programs, and unnecessary junk? If so, you realize that as a result of being overloaded, your computer works slower and slower, perhaps finally giving up the ghost and refusing to work altogether. Your GI tract can suffer a shutdown in a similar way as a result of overloading it with too much "junk" food. When people consistently overeat, stuffing themselves into misery, they are placing an enormous strain on their GI tract. Even worse, many people do their overeating late at night, which does not allow the GI tract to rest even when you go to bed; it is still digesting all that "food."

The small intestine has been designed for several

major functions to maintain your health. It acts as an organ of digestion and absorption of nutrients to fuel your body's energy level. It also acts as a protective barrier to keep your body from absorbing toxic materials and other undesirable matter, such as large molecules of undigested food.

A healthy small intestine allows ready absorption of needed nutrients such as *triglycerides* from the digestion of fats, *sugars* from the digestion of carbohydrates, *amino acids* and *di-* and *tri-peptides* from the digestion of proteins—all vital compounds needed to ensure your health. It also seals out toxins, heavy metals, undigested bits of food, and other matter that could cause your body harm.

Health problems begin when we abuse our digestive system's natural functions in such ways as consuming anti-inflammatory medications, aspirin, alcohol, and certain other substances in excess, which can irritate and inflame the lining of your intestines. This irritation can lead to microscopic openings and holes in the small intestine, which allow harmful matter such as toxins and partially digested foods to pass into your blood stream. This unhealthy condition is called *increased intestinal permeability*.

Increased intestinal permeability allows toxins and other harmful substances to enter the bloodstream and eventually become lodged in the liver, causing major disruptions in its healthy function. These foreign substances undermine the efficient detoxification processes of the liver and trigger the release of free radicals, as I have mentioned, which damage the liver as well as other organs and tissues throughout the body. Increased intestinal permeability is often the root cause of food allergies or food sensitivities, inflammatory bowel disease such as ulcerative colitis, Crohn's disease, chronic skin problems, and other serious health conditions.

In order to improve intestinal health, I recommend that, in addition to using the detoxification and fasting program presented in this book, you do the following:

- Always avoid overeating.
- You should reinoculate the bowel with friendly bacteria: lactobacillus acidophilus for the small intestines and bifido bacteria for the large intestine. These good bacteria can also help prevent damage to the lining of the GI tract, thus maintaining normal intestinal permeability.
- Refrain from eating before bedtime.
- Determine to decrease the stress in your life, especially when eating, by choosing to eat in a relaxed, peaceful atmosphere.

Enjoy increased energy and better health.

A wonderful benefit from cleansing the body through proper fasting is increased energy levels. Cellular toxins and free radicals impair the mitochondria (the energy factories in each cell), hindering them from producing energy effectively. As a result, you may suffer fatigue, irritability, and lethargy. When you fast, you allow your cells to shed many toxins so they can again produce the energy you need.

Short-term fasting will also boost your immune system, which will help prevent disease and illness and give you a longer life. Along with an improved quality of life, you will discover that fasting even makes you look better. Your skin will eventually become clearer, giving you a radiance you have not known since your youth. The whites of your eyes will usually become clearer—they may even sparkle.

Melting away toxic fat through fasting will help you feel and look better than you have in years. Along with increased energy, you will most likely enjoy improved mental functioning as your body cleanses, repairs, and rejuvenates every organ, including your brain.

Physical Benefits for Specific Diseases

Especially when you are sick or diseased, your body is signaling that you need to rest from your work and other activities. In the case of certain diseases, it is also trying to communicate to you the need to rest from foods, especially those that are difficult to digest. Not only can fasting *prevent* sickness by allowing the body to rest and cleanse itself, but fasting also has amazing healing benefits for people who are already suffering illness and disease. From minor ailments such as colds and flu to the life-threatening symptoms of heart disease, fasting holds powerful benefits for healing the body. I have listed some important considerations for specific diseases regarding the special benefits received through fasting.

Colds and flu

Did you know that symptoms of colds and flu are worsened by the way we eat when we are sick? For example, drinking coffee and sodas as well as eating ice cream and other sweets can make your flu or cold symptoms worse. Instead, if you fast by drinking plenty of water and fresh juices, while getting lots of rest, you will help your body expel toxic materials through the mucus it creates. Fever also has a healing effect, designed to activate your immune system. (Of course, a high fever or a fever that persists for more than a few days requires examination by a physician.)

Simply by eliminating mucus-forming foods such as dairy products, eggs, and processed grains (pancakes, processed cereals, doughnuts, white bread, crackers, and so forth), you can overcome many infectious diseases. Also, plan to eliminate from your diet margarine as well as partially hydrogenated, hydrogenated, and processed oils. A small amount of organic butter may be consumed after the illness. In the early 1900s, Professor Arnold Ehret targeted the ill effects of these mucus-forming foods and developed a "Mucusless Diet Healing System" that proved to be very healing for the body.[1]

I recommend that you do not automatically run to the doctor for antibiotics every time you have a cold or flu. It is much better to let your body's own immune system be your first defense against infections. As I mentioned earlier, there are negatives to overusing antibiotics, like yeast overgrowth as well as an increased toxic burden on the liver. And doctors sometimes prescribe antibiotics for symptoms that do not respond to antibiotics. Unless you have a fever of 101 degrees for a few days, you probably don't need to see your doctor. Even if you do, don't insist on antibiotics unless recommended by your physician.

Autoimmune diseases

Diseases caused by the body's immune system attacking itself are referred to as autoimmune diseases. A military term for this phenomenon is the tragedy of "friendly fire," when casualties are caused by a person's own comrades. When your immune system becomes confused (as in autoimmune diseases), it cannot distinguish between normal cells and invader cells. So it produces antibodies that actually attack its own healthy tissues, inflaming, damaging and sometimes even destroying the tissue.

Poor digestion, increased intestinal permeability, and increased meat consumption contribute to increased risk of autoimmune disease. Your stomach and pancreas simply do not produce enough hydrochloric acid and enzymes to properly digest the quantities of meat typical to the American diet. Inadequate amounts of hydrochloric acid and enzymes are produced to break down the proteins into the individual amino acids needed for properly digesting such quantities of meat. Instead, incompletely digested proteins, called *peptides,* are formed, which may be directly passed into the bloodstream, especially if you already suffer from increased intestinal permeability.

Then your immune system may begin to form antibodies to attack these peptides in the bloodstream. Unfortunately, sometimes the immune system becomes confused and cannot distinguish between a foreign invader and its own healthy cells. That is when the body may start to attack itself, creating inflammation and disease.

Add to this the high levels of stress most people endure from our modern lifestyles, which reduce the quantity of hydrochloric acid and pancreatic enzymes available for digestion, and you understand the result of our diet and lifestyle, reflected in the current epidemic of indigestion, bloating, and excessive gas. Only the pharmaceutical companies stand to profit from our national health dilemma—and they are making a killing!

Diseases such as rheumatoid arthritis and lupus are rare in countries in Asia, such as Japan and China, and countries in Africa, where people eat mostly fruits, vegetables, and whole grains. Yet, even in these cultures, people who adopt our western diet begin to develop more autoimmune diseases.

Fasting, especially juice fasting, is very beneficial in reversing autoimmune diseases. Some physicians have had outstanding results as well with water fasting. However, if you are suffering from an autoimmune disease, it will be extremely important that you wean yourself off all medications, under the watchful medical supervision of your physician, and that you allow your physician to carefully monitor your fasting therapy.

After fasting, patients with autoimmune disease should determine to change their eating patterns, also. For more information regarding autoimmune diseases, refer to my book *The Bible Cure for Auto-immune Diseases.*

Hypertension

If you are suffering from high blood pressure, you must allow your physician to professionally wean you off all medications before attempting a short fast, just as patients with autoimmune disease do. One of the most effective treatments for hypertension is a juice fast. Also, increase your water consumption to two or three quarts of filtered water a day. I recommend that you follow the directions for the detoxification fast outlined in this book. (See Appendix A.) There is also helpful information available to you in my book *The Bible Cure for High Blood Pressure.*

Coronary disease

It has been proven by doctors like Dean Ornish that coronary artery disease can be reversed with a vegetarian diet, stress management, and exercise.[2] After only a year on his program, Dr. Ornish's patients had much less plaque in their arteries. If you have significant coronary artery disease or suffer from peripheral vascular disease, which is plaque buildup in the lower extremities, I recommend that you follow the Mediterranean diet as described in my book *What Would Jesus Eat?*

Regular, periodic fasting is also very effective in the treatment of these diseases, helping to remove plaque from the arteries. During a fast, you may find that your cholesterol levels actually become more elevated. This is only a sign that the fast is working, breaking down the plaque and releasing it into the bloodstream so that it can be effectively removed, so don't be alarmed.

Again, it is important that your physician monitor your fast, checking blood work before your fast, during your fast, and at the completion of your fast.

Psoriasis and eczema

Because many patients with psoriasis or eczema also suffer from food allergies, it is extremely important when choosing a juice fast that they drink only juices from foods to which they are not allergic. If necessary, the patient should have food allergy testing first. More helpful information is available in my book *The Bible Cure for Skin Disorders*. These patients usually suffer from increased intestinal permeability and impaired liver function as well. If you suffer from psoriasis or eczema, it will be necessary to repair your GI tract and detoxify your liver before choosing to fast. Follow the program outlined in Appendix A.

It is likely that you suffer from yeast overgrowth in the intestinal tract. If this is the case, it will be important to follow a diet specially designed to improve this candida overgrowth condition for at least three months before you begin your fast. My books *The Bible Cure for Candida and Yeast Infections* and *The Bible Cure Recipes for Overcoming Candida* will give you helpful information as well.

MY TESTIMONY

One morning approximately fifteen years ago, I awoke with itching of my arms and legs. The itching was so intense I thought that I might have contracted scabies from one of my patients. Shortly, I developed a red scaly rash, which eventually covered my hands, arms, and legs. Many times the rash would burn as if a lighted match were touching my skin; other times it would itch so intensely that I would claw at my skin in my sleep. I would awaken to find blood on my sheets from my scratching. As a result, I developed sores on my arms, elbows, hands, and legs. I wondered if leprosy could be any worse than this.

My patients would ask me repeatedly what had caused my horrible skin condition. So I tried to cover it up by wearing long-sleeve shirts. However, I was unable to conceal my hands, and they would observe the horrible sores on my hands and fingers, asking the same questions. Looking for help, I began to study advanced nutrition and detoxification. I then implemented these powerful truths in my own life.

First, I experimented to discover which foods were triggering my condition, making it worse. I found that nightshade vegetables would aggravate my condition. These include tomatoes, potatoes, eggplant, and peppers. Every time I ate a nightshade vegetable, my psoriasis condition flared up. Strangely, it was these foods that I craved on a daily basis. I especially loved salsa, tomatoes, and potatoes. For most people, these foods are healthy foods to consume; however, for me these foods were actually aggravating my psoriasis.

The worst triggers for me were fried foods, hydrogenated and partially hydrogenated fats, and processed polyunsaturated fats. I realized that every time I ate a salad with a commercial salad dressing, my psoriasis would flare. But I found I was able to consume extra-virgin olive oil without any problem. Another trigger that worsened my condition was red meat and pork, especially bacon, so I eliminated these from my diet. Finally, I realized that another major trigger was stress. When I was under more stress and felt overwhelmed, the psoriasis flared up.

As I discovered these nutritional and lifestyle triggers to this terrible skin condition, I began to adjust my eating and add helpful nutrients to my diet. Along with extra-virgin olive oil, I began supplementing my diet with essential fats in the form of pharmaceutical-grade fish oil and evening primrose oil. I took supplements to repair my GI tract and began to reintroduce large quantities of good bacteria into it as well. For more information on the nutritional therapies helpful to overcoming psoriasis, please refer to my book *The Bible Cure for Skin Disorders.*

Though my psoriasis condition cleared up by following strict nutritional guidelines, I found that my diet was very restrictive. I could never eat tomatoes without suffering a flare-up, and I love tomatoes. That is when I began to investigate the healing power of fasting personally.

After completing a seven-day fast, supplementing the fast with milk thistle and dandelion tea, not only did my psoriasis completely clear up, but also I was able to begin eating foods that would ordinarily have triggered the condition. I only eat these trigger foods in moderation, once or twice a week, but I have been successful in adding them to my diet without any further flare-ups since the fast. And my greatest joy is that I have been able to help literally hundreds of patients overcome psoriasis by implementing these same principles in their lives. I also recommend desensitization to food allergies by NAET. For more information, please refer to *The Bible Cure for Allergies.*

Allergies and asthma

Allergies, whether airborne or food allergies, usually improve dramatically during a fast, and sometimes even disappear. The reason is that there is a close connection between allergies and the toxic condition of the liver as well as to increased intestinal permeability. During a fast, the digestive tract has time to rest and repair itself, which also helps the liver to detoxify.

Of course, it is important that you consume juices from foods to which you are not allergic. It may be helpful to keep a journal while you are fasting. (See Appendix C.) Note any adverse reactions and refer to the juices you consumed prior to the allergic reaction, avoiding them for the rest of the fast.

MY WIFE'S TESTIMONY

For years my wife, Mary, has suffered from severe allergies with continual bouts of sneezing, itching, weeping eyes, postnasal drip on a daily basis, and a chronic hacking cough. I could actually locate my wife in any large department store simply by following the sound of her constant hacking cough; it became a natural honing device when I wanted to find her. My wife's weeping eyes were so severe from allergies that people would ask her why she was crying.

About four years ago, Mary decided to go on a five-day fast. Amazingly, after that fast, all of her allergy symptoms went away. She no longer experienced the bouts of sneezing, the itchy weeping eyes, the postnasal drip, or the chronic hacking cough. These symptoms have not returned to this day.

Type 2 diabetes

Fasting is extremely effective for Type 2 diabetics. (Please note that Type 1 diabetics should NOT fast.) Type 2 diabetics usually suffer from obesity and usually have high insulin levels. The cells are resistant to the insulin because the insulin receptors on the surfaces of these cells do not function properly. For that reason, these patients should not fast using fruits or vegetables with high glycemic indexes, such as carrot juice. I recommend they fast using a well-balanced, high-fiber protein supplement called UltraGlycemX by Metagenics. (See Appendix D.)

Another excellent product that can help diabetics' fasting programs is called *Living Fuel*. This product is a powdered form of juiced vegetables and protein designed to detoxify the body and repair a damaged metabolism by removing the stress of everyday foods and providing everything the body needs to thrive in a restricted caloric format. (See Appendix D for more information.)

It is also very important for diabetics to have an aerobic exercise program and to eat a low glycemic diet. You will find more helpful information regarding diabetes in my book *The Bible Cure for Diabetes*.

It has been my experience that overweight patients are able to follow a strict diet for a short time.

After that, they begin to splurge and binge, eating the wrong kinds of food. Periodic short fasts help you to crucify your fleshly desires for overeating, diminishing these unhealthy desires for food, which is the key to gaining control over your body that can last a lifetime. If you need help to lose weight and keep it off, I recommend that you read my book *The Bible Cure for Weight Loss and Muscle Gain.*

Crohn's disease and ulcerative colitis

For patients suffering from Crohn's disease and ulcerative colitis, fasting can be very healing. These diseases are usually characterized by increased intestinal permeability, a toxic liver, food allergies, and candida overgrowth. These patients are usually extremely sensitive to all forms of sugar and dairy products, which should be totally eliminated from the diet. Because of this sensitivity, they should not try to fast with fruit or vegetable juices, which contain natural sugars. Usually, these patients do best on either a balanced rice protein such as UltraClear Plus by Metagenics or on a water fast.

It is important to continue eating healthy rice products—primarily brown rice, brown rice bread, and rice crackers—once your fast is over. Eat a primarily vegetarian diet, slowly reintroducing small amounts of protein. And keep a food diary to find out what foods cause food sensitivities, avoiding any that irritate your GI tract. For more information, please refer to my books *The Bible Cure for Autoimmune Diseases* and *The Bible Cure for Candida and Yeast Infections*. You may also want to consider eating according to the blood-type diet. (See Appendix D for resources.)

Caution: When You Should NOT Fast

There are health conditions and other situations that prohibit fasting for certain individuals. While the following list is not exhaustive, it does include some major conditions that will not allow you to fast. Please consult your physician before considering a fast, regardless of your state of health. However, if you have any of the following, DO NOT fast:

- Do not fast if you are pregnant or nursing.
- Do not fast if you are extremely debilitated or malnourished, which would include patients with cancer, AIDS, severe anemia, or any severe wasting conditions.
- Do not fast before or after surgery, since it may interfere with your ability to heal after surgery.
- Do not fast if you suffer from cardiac arrhythmia or congestive heart failure.
- Do not fast if you are struggling with mental illness, including schizophrenia, bipolar disorder, major depression, and severe anxiety.

- Do not fast if you suffer from severe liver and kidney disease.
- Do not fast if you are a Type 1 diabetic.
- Do not fast if you are taking anti-inflammatory medications, aspirin, antidepressants, narcotics, chemotherapy, or diuretics. (Medications such as thyroid hormones and hormone replacement therapy are safe to take during a fast. Always consult your physician before fasting if you are taking any medication.)
- Do not fast if you are taking prednisone. You will need to first wean off this medication slowly under doctor's supervision. (You may continue to take low doses of hypertension medications during a fast as long as you are monitored by a physician. However, this does not include diuretics.)

As a physician, I try to help wean my patients off most of their medications prior to supervising a fast for them. I am not recommending to anyone that you fast except under your physician's supervision.

Chapter 3

MENTAL AND SPIRITUAL
BENEFITS OF FASTING

I believe fasting is a key to genuine and deep spirituality. History reveals that those who sought to know God and desired to experience spiritual realms and divine giftings employed fasting as a powerful and important tool in their pursuit. Bible heroes also practiced fasting to release the power of God into their lives and situations. Biblical fasting involves voluntarily abstaining from food for a period of time for a *spiritual purpose.*

Denying yourself one of the most basic elements of survival, one that is loved and cherished by your body and that brings psychological pleasure as well, for a length of time humbles your body and mind, resulting in a strengthening of your spirit. Two words used in the Old Testament that are translated as *fasting* involve the following meanings: "to cover the mouth" and "to humble oneself."

Humbling the "Flesh"

Fasting is a way of showing your destructive, fleshly desires who is "boss." The Bible refers to the base desires of our body and mind as the "flesh." It instructs us to overcome these desires and allow the Spirit of God, who resides in the spirit of born-again believers, to rule our lives. As powerful as the lower nature can appear, fasting humbles it, breaking its destructive power. Fasting is a key to humility, which brings the favor of God on our lives. The Scriptures instruct us to seek humility:

> Be clothed with humility, for "God resists the proud, but gives grace to the humble." Therefore humble yourselves under the mighty hand of God, that He may exalt you in due time.
>
> —1 Peter 5:5–6, nkjv

Arrogance is a result of always getting what we think we deserve. As long as we pamper our flesh, giving in to its inordinate desires, it becomes more demanding in its prideful ways. Humbling our flesh through fasting, according to Scripture, will bring us into favor with God, who gives grace to those who humble themselves before Him. It is not the work of God to make us humble; He tells us to humble ourselves. As we choose to humble ourselves with fasting and prayer, God comes to our aid and reveals His love, purposes, and plans for our individual lives, and even for nations, as the Bible records.

Regaining Control

How many of you have discovered the strength of your natural appetites for things that are not good for you? Whether it is the carnal appetite for overeating, sugar, gossip, inappropriate sex, or other inordinate desires, these strong cravings are part of our base nature, which the Bible calls "flesh." While God intended for our spirits to rule our minds and bodies, too often we have to admit that our bodies and minds are vying for control.

For example, instead of spending time in prayer, our minds scream for one more TV program. When the bathroom scale tells us we need to drop a few pounds, we cannot say *no* to one more slice of chocolate cake or bowl of ice cream. When that happens, we must admit that our flesh is dominating our spirits, making wrong choices that will hinder our health and our lives in God.

It is a fact that fasting is a powerful way to break the grip of these base desires that rule our lives, allowing the spirit to regain the control it was intended to have over our lives. Our relationship with God, who is Spirit, depends on our communing with Him through our spirits by the power of the Holy Spirit who dwells in every believer. Fasting "feeds" our spirit man, starving the natural desires at the same time. Amazingly, it softens the heart while cleansing the body, making us more receptive to God's plans. It is remarkable how clearly our spirits can discern the voice and internal promptings of God's Spirit when the "screaming voices" of the body and mind have been subdued through fasting.

The Scriptures clearly teach restraint of gluttonous appetites: "When you sit down to eat with a ruler, consider carefully what is before you; and put a knife to your throat if you are a man given to appetite. Do not desire his delicacies, for they are deceptive food" (Prov. 23:1–3, NKJV). The king's dainties were delicacies that probably consisted of high-sugar foods. Consider the following prominent "desires of the flesh" that should be controlled:

- Lethargy or apathy that resists the thought of exercise
- Cravings for the wrong kinds of foods, such as sugary foods and fats, which cause obesity without giving proper nourishment
- Emotional outbursts that make us "out-of-control," such as anger and rage that prompt us to say hurtful things to our loved ones or to have frenzied reactions to traffic delays

Other inordinate desires of the flesh include cravings for inappropriate sex, a compulsion to binge on any kind of food, becoming a "couch potato" for TV or video games, and so forth. Undisciplined wants and cravings define the phrase "desires of the flesh." And they have a destructive power over our bodies, minds, and spiritual lives, as demonstrated in the epidemic of unnecessary degenerative diseases that plague our nation.

Regaining control of our lives from the effect of fleshly desires is possible as we learn to embrace the biblical principle of fasting. The Scriptures teach that we are in a war within ourselves between our spirits and our flesh. The apostle Paul declares:

> For those who live according to the flesh set their minds on the things of the flesh, but those who live according to the Spirit, the things of the Spirit. For to be carnally minded is death, but to be spiritually minded is life and peace. Because the carnal mind is enmity against God; for it is not subject to the law of God, nor indeed can be.
>
> —ROMANS 8:5–7, NKJV

As long as we obey the desires of our carnal mind, we will break the laws of God, which, according to this scripture, results in death. While this scripture may have a broader application, it can certainly be applied to the negative physical, mental, and spiritual results that living an undisciplined life will bring. God expects us to be good stewards of the gift of life

He has given us, especially as believers. The apostle Paul also challenged believers to acknowledge that their bodies are the temples of God and should not be defiled (1 Cor. 3:16–17).

What is the answer to this natural dilemma of "fleshly desires"? Again, the Bible gives a clear answer: "I say then: Walk in the Spirit, and you shall not fulfill the lust of the flesh. For the flesh lusts [wars] against the Spirit, and the Spirit against the flesh; and these are contrary to one another" (Gal. 5:16–17, NKJV). As we choose to subdue the flesh through fasting, our spirits can regain control and have power to overcome fleshly desires, which will result in life and health: physically, mentally, and spiritually.

Enhancing Mental Health

When stress plays a major role in your life, as it does in most Americans, it hinders your digestive processes, endangering your health. Many stressed-out individuals have stomach medications strewed all around their workplace and car. Stress can cause a deficiency in hydrochloric acid as well as pancreatic enzymes so necessary to digestion. These deficiencies cause poor digestion of proteins, fats, and carbohydrates. When this happens, partially digested food can putrefy as it travels through your GI tract, causing various kinds of health problems.

Beating the effects of stress

Don't eat when you are stressed. Consciously choose to relax a bit before you pick up your fork. Take a minute to breathe deeply and begin to consider reasons you have to be thankful, simply for the gift of life. This need to relax before eating is a good reason to express gratitude to God for His provision of your food and other blessings. These positive thoughts will have a wonderful therapeutic effect on your digestive system.

If you eat when you are upset, angry, or fearful, such negative emotions will stimulate the sympathetic nervous system, which will result in a decreased secretion of hydrochloric acid so vital to digestion. This results in reducing the secretions of pancreatic enzymes, making it very difficult to digest proteins, fats, and carbohydrates. When poor digestion occurs, it may lead to increased intestinal permeability, which I discussed earlier, allowing putrefying food to enter your bloodstream and wreak havoc with your detox system.

Fasting allows the body and mind even greater power to recover from these stress-induced conditions. Without pouring more food into a struggling digestive system, the body is free to begin to do housecleaning of the putrefaction that has accumulated, even in the brain. And in turn, a properly working digestive system helps to relieve the agitation of body and mind caused by toxins floating around in the brain as well as the entire body.

Overcoming depression

Toxins overloading the body can also cause mental and emotional depression. As we have mentioned, our daily exposure to toxins in our food, water, and air allows our body to absorb heavy metals, solvents, pesticides, and other environmental toxins. When these toxins are stored in our brain and other centers of the nervous system, they can create such a toxic burden that we eventually develop fatigue, depression, and anxiety.

Caffeine and excessive sugar intake are linked to depression. Excessive intake of these two items alone can lead to a loss of B vitamins, an increase in the stress hormone cortisol, and sleep disturbances. The combination of deficiency of these vitamins, along with an excess of cortisol in the system and inadequate sleep, is a recipe for depression. If you feel you may be suffering from major depression, please refer to my book *Deadly Emotions*.

Ridding the body of an excessive overload of toxins through fasting can greatly reduce symptoms of depression and anxiety. For more information on overcoming depression and anxiety, please refer to my book *The Bible Cure for Depression and Anxiety*.

Enjoying peace

Many people testify to a restful peace in their bodies as well as their minds, especially when they eliminate for a while the more toxic foods that cripple their digestive systems and hinder the work of the immune system as well. The Bible confirms this mental and spiritual health benefit from fasting.

For example, after Jesus fasted for forty days in the wilderness, the tempter (the devil) came to tempt Him. According to the victorious response Jesus gave the devil, it is obvious that Jesus was strengthened in His mind and spirit, even though He would have been weakened in His body from His fast. He was able to answer the devil with the written Word and conquer all His temptations. (See Matthew 4.) And the scriptures declare that after gaining this wonderful victory over the devil, Jesus "returned in the power of the Spirit to Galilee, and news of Him went out through all the surrounding region" (Luke 4:14, NKJV). The power of the Spirit of God was released in the life of Christ as a result of His obedience through fasting.

Building Godly Character

The good news for all born-again believers is that it is possible to be led by the Spirit of God and not ruled by destructive fleshly desires. The apostle Paul is one of the best examples of a life that was led by the Spirit. His attitude toward the fleshly desires that militated against his life is reflected in Scripture:

> And every man that striveth for the mastery is temperate in all things....I therefore so run, not as uncertainly; so fight I, not as one that beateth the air: But I keep under my body, and bring it into subjection.
>
> —1 CORINTHIANS 9:25–27, KJV

> But in all things we commend ourselves as ministers of God: in much patience, in tribulations, in needs, in distresses...in fastings.
>
> —2 CORINTHIANS 6:4–5, NKJV

Through fasting we are enabled to surrender our lives to God more fully. As a result, we find we have more control over our tongues, our minds, our attitudes, our emotions, our bodies, and all our fleshly desires. Our spirits are released more fully to embrace the laws and will of God and to allow us to fulfill His purposes for our lives.

The desires of the flesh lose their power as we "starve" them, focusing upon the Spirit of God through prayer and reading of His Word. Our minds are renewed with the truth of God's Word, and the promises and positive attitudes He reveals become our focus. Our thoughts will be filled with the power of God to resist negative, poisonous emotions and attitudes. When we fill our minds with God's words and thoughts through the reading of the Bible and through prayer, we feed and strengthen our spirit man, which desires to please God. The way to die to fleshly desires and to build godly character is to spend time in the presence of God. Fasting enables us to die to the inordinate appetites of our lower nature, the lusts of the flesh.

Releasing God's power

There are many instances recorded in Scripture of God's supernatural intervention in individual lives and in nations when His people humbled themselves through prayer and fasting. Moses fasted for forty days as he waited in God's presence on the mountain and received the law of God for Israel. Daniel fasted and prayed twenty-one days for his nation, seeking God to fulfill His promise to deliver them from captivity, which was accomplished. The early church "ministered to the Lord and fasted," and God revealed His will for lives of individual ministers (Acts 13:1–3, NKJV). The spiritual power released through fasting will enable us to touch the world around us with God's love and power.

And there is a scriptural promise of healing through fasting. The prophet Isaiah recorded the acceptable fast

unto the Lord, which involves more than simply denying ourselves food for a time; it involves a change in
attitude and showing compassion to the needy as well.
When we do that, God promises, "Then your light will
break out like the dawn, and your recovery will speedily spring forth; and your righteousness will go before
you" (Isa. 58:8). Releasing the healing power of God in
our lives as we subdue the destructive appetites of the
flesh is a wonderful benefit of spiritual fasting.

Regular Spiritual Fasting

Not only does Scripture advocate spiritual fasting, but
it also indicates that it should be a regular part of the
believer's life. Jesus Himself taught us how to fast spiritually with the right motivation:

> And whenever you fast, do not put on a gloomy
> face as the hypocrites do, for they neglect their
> appearance in order to be seen fasting by men.
> Truly I say to you, they have their reward in full.
> But you, when you fast, anoint your head, and
> wash your face so that you may not be seen fasting
> by men, but by your Father who is in secret; and
> your Father who sees in secret will repay you.
> —MATTHEW 6:16–18

We know that Jewish leaders fasted regularly
(Luke 18:12). And Jesus made it clear that *when* we
fast, not *if*, we are to be motivated to please God and

not to receive honor from men. He promised that God will openly reward those who fast with the right motivation. While the Scriptures do not impose strict rules as to when we should fast or how often, we can be led by the Spirit into seasons of fasting.

According to historical church documents like the *Didache*, written in the second century, we understand that the church actually ordered regular weekly fasts on Wednesdays and Fridays.[1] While this may have promoted legalism in the matter of fasting, which we want to avoid, it does show the importance the church placed on following Jesus' command to fast. Throughout history, church leaders have promoted fasting. Martin Luther, leader of the Protestant reformation, encouraged voluntary and private fasting. The Catholic church set aside Friday as its fast day. John Wesley advocated the two fast days outlined in the *Didache*, refusing to ordain Methodist ministers who did not comply.

However you choose to make fasting a part of your lifestyle, it is important that you do so to enjoy the spiritual benefits I have mentioned. And it is vital that you be motivated to please God and die to your carnal desires in order to receive the blessings God promises to those who fast, including physical, mental, and spiritual health. I strongly recommend that you keep a fasting journal to record the wonderful blessings and benefits you experience from your fasts. (See Appendix C.)

Having concluded that fasting is beneficial for all areas of our lives, I trust you are ready to decide to make fasting a regular part of your lifestyle. In order to do that effectively, you will want to know how to fast, when to fast, how long to fast, and other practical matters regarding a healthy approach to fasting. Get ready to experience the wonderful benefits of fasting as you read the next chapters carefully to determine how to begin.

Chapter 4

HOW SHOULD I FAST?

As a physician, I have closely examined many popular methods of fasting. I have found some to be very beneficial and others to be quite dangerous. So, to help you decide how to fast, let me review a few of the fasting methods people have developed and then discuss the method I am convinced will put you on a path to healthier living.

Total Fasting

Some people consider fasting to be a period of time during which *nothing* is taken by mouth, including no food and no water. Perhaps this is a technically correct definition of a total fast; however, it is too extreme to be safe for most people. I never recommend total fasting.

Because your body must have at least two quarts of water every day to sustain healthy life, it is dangerous to go even a few days without drinking water. Many people do not normally drink the adequate amount of water they need to be healthy. Their lack of proper hydration of their body results in various health conditions caused simply by dehydration. Attempting to go without water for any period of time can be extremely harmful to the body. For this reason, I do not recommend a total fast without water.

A Water-Only Fast

The next strictest form of fasting is to eat no foods and drink no liquids except for water for a period of time. I do not usually recommend this type of fasting, either. The only exception would be for certain autoimmune diseases such as lupus and rheumatoid arthritis or severe atherosclerosis, which usually respond very favorably to a short, water-only fast. However, such a fast must be done under the direct supervision and monitoring of your physician. Similar benefits for these diseases can also be experienced more safely with juice fasting; it just takes longer.

Anyone who desires to fast with water only must be prepared to devote several days to doing little more than resting; water-only fasting weakens the body so that working a full-time job during the fast would be impossible for most individuals. Unless you are suffering from a specific disease that could benefit from a few days of water-only fasting, I recommend that you consider the fast presented here—juice fasting. A juice fast gives the same benefits without the unpleasant weakness and hunger that often accompany water-only fasting.

A Partial Fast

Many people who are not able to use the above methods of fasting choose to fast partially, using the biblical hero Daniel as their model. During a time of captivity, the young Israelite Daniel and his friends were carried to the king's court because they were "good-looking, showing intelligence in every branch of wisdom, endowed with understanding, and discerning knowledge, and who had ability for serving in the king's court" (Dan. 1:4). There the king demanded that they eat a daily provision of the king's meat and drink the king's wine for three years in order to prepare them to serve in the king's court. This diet would have meant defiling the conscience of these Jewish youth (probably because this food would have been dedicated to idols), and Daniel and his friends determined not to do so.

Matthew Henry comments that Daniel requested, "Prove us for ten days; during that time let us have nothing but pulse to eat, nothing but herbs and fruits, or parched peas or lentils, and nothing but water to drink, and see how we can live upon that, and proceed accordingly."[1] They were granted their request, and after ten days their countenances appeared fairer and fatter in flesh than all the young men who ate the portion of the king's meat (Dan. 1:15).

The plan was for these young men to be nourished in this way for three years before they appeared before the king. And the Scriptures declare that at the end of those three years, when they appeared before the king, Daniel, Shadrach, Meshach, and Abednego were ten times better than all the magicians and astrologers in wisdom and understanding. (See Daniel 1:20.) Matthew Henry comments further: "People will not believe the benefit of abstemiousness and a spare diet, nor how much it contributes to the health of the body, unless they try it."[2] This biblical example reinforces the tremendous power of living, natural foods instead of dead, devitalized "dainties."

According to this biblical model, a *partial fast* would probably consist of freshly cooked vegetables and fresh fruit, perhaps with some brown rice, legumes, and soups. It would eliminate all highly caloric, sugary foods, meats, and any type of caffeinated beverages along with modern junk foods.

Juice Fasting

I recommend a safer, more effective complete detoxification method of fasting—juice fasting. Some who recommend the more severe forms of fasting do not consider juice fasting a true method of fasting. And some do not feel juice fasting brings the same benefits, spiritually or physically, as a water-only fast.

As a medical doctor, I have experienced the physical benefits, as well as powerful spiritual benefits, of juice fasting for my patients and myself many times. I believe motivation is a very important part of fasting, no matter what regimen you choose, that determines much of the outcome.

I have referenced the water-only fast as beneficial, especially for certain diseases. However, juice fasting can be even more beneficial because of its detoxification support, its effect of restoring the body's alkaline level, and the support it gives to the liver. Juice fasting is also far less strenuous, usually not causing the typical weakness or hunger of a water-only fast; a person can actually experience tremendous new levels of energy during a juice fast.

While water-only fasting can reduce inflammation in the body and actually cause the hardened arterial plaque of severe coronary disease to regress or melt away, juice fasting can produce a similar effect over a more extended period of time. And there are other important health benefits that accompany the method of juice fasting.

Restoring delicate health balance

You may not be aware that the health of your body is based upon a delicate natural acid/alkaline balance. Maintaining this balance is necessary for your body to detoxify successfully. If you are eating the standard American diet (SAD), filled with sugars, fats, and too much protein, your tissues will become more acidic than nature intended. What happens when your body becomes too acidic?

In a sense, your cells become "constipated," filled with waste that they cannot adequately get rid of. With this condition of acidity, the energy-producing structures in the cell (mitochondria) do not function properly, resulting in a lack of energy and fatigue. Free-radical activity also increases as the toxic overload continues to build, which results in your body's deterioration and degenerative diseases.

In order to determine the level of acidity of your body, you can purchase some pH strips at the drugstore. Collect the first morning urine and dip a pH paper into it. The change of color of the strip will indicate your urine's pH level, which can be matched to a numerical reading. If your pH test reading is 5.0, your body is very acidic. A normal reading would be between 6.5 and 7.5. A pH reading of 5.0 indicates your body is one hundred times more acidic than a person with a pH of 7.0. Periodic juice fasting is very effective in bringing back this important acid/alkaline balance so that the cells can begin to excrete toxins again. Before discussing in more detail the benefits of juice fasting, please review the following list of other fasting "boundaries" that will bring powerful physical as well as spiritual results to your life.

Fasting Boundaries

There are many different kinds of fasting—and they don't always involve abstaining from food. Take a look at the following list to give you some ideas:

- A partial fast as in the biblical example of Daniel (Dan. 1)
- A water fast (do not go over three days unless monitored by a doctor)
- A fruit and vegetable juice fast (as discussed in this book)
- A fast with a powdered protein supplement (such as UltraGlycemX, UltraClear Plus, or Living Fuel)
- A word fast (a refusal to speak any words that hurt, injure, or cause fear, doubt, anger, strife, shame or guilt). This fast will help you as a mother or father to use language that is courteous, kind, and uplifting to your family.
- A media fast (eliminating TV, Internet, radio, and other forms of entertainment in order to listen to the Bible on tape as well as devotional materials, teaching tapes, and so forth). The media fast is one of the most important kinds of fasts. Do not watch TV or listen to the news for one week. Instead,

spend that time fellowshiping with family and friends, reading the Bible, and praying.

- A fast from gossip. This fast helps you gain control over such deadly, toxic social environments as negativity at work or with a social group. Refuse to gossip or listen to gossip.
- A fast from other areas of personal addiction that you want to have broken over your life, including (fill in the blank) _____

_____

_____

Special Precautions for Special Health Issues

If your state of health is less than desirable at present, you may reap great benefits from fasting. However, you should also take special precautions to address your health issues before considering a fast. The following health issues require some attention to ensure that fasting will be beneficial, not harmful.

Candidiasis, food allergies, parasites

If you experience symptoms of excessive bloating, gas, and diarrhea, you may be suffering from candidiasis, bacterial overgrowth in the small intestines, or even a parasitic infection. These symptoms may also signal malabsorption, maldigestion, increased intestinal permeability, or food allergies. If you have any of these symptoms, I strongly recommend that you get a comprehensive digestive stool analysis with parasitology, a test for intestinal permeability, and a food allergy test before you decide to fast. (See Appendix D.) In addition, I recommend that you read my book *The Bible Cure for Candida and Yeast Infections* and follow the special diet it contains for three months before you start fasting.

Hypoglycemia

If you suffer from hypoglycemia, you need to maintain a constant blood sugar level by drinking juice every two or three hours while fasting, instead of only four or five times a day. Also, I recommend that you grind 1 tablespoon of flaxseed and add it to your juice daily as a source of fiber. You may choose another source of fiber instead, such as rice bran, psyllium seeds or husks, and oat bran, which are very good as well.

Adrenal fatigue is commonly associated with hypoglycemia. My book *The Bible Cure for Stress* recommends supplements for this condition.

GI tract sensitivities

Some who suffer from sensitive GI tract symptoms, such as pain, bloating, gas, or diarrhea after drinking a certain kind of juice, simply need to omit that fruit or vegetable and try a different one. By process of elimination, you will be able to identify the fruit or vegetable to which your GI tract is sensitive and then avoid using it in your fast. Also, some patients with sensitive GI tracts show less symptoms when they separate vegetable and fruit juices, instead of drinking them in combination.

Another approach for people who suffer from GI tract sensitivities is to choose fruits and vegetables that are compatible with their blood type. You can find out your blood type by donating blood at the local blood bank or by going to your doctor. If you are unfamiliar with the concept of eating according to your blood type, I recommend that you read the books *Eat Right for Your Type* by Peter J. D'Adamo, ND and *Bloodtypes, Bodytypes and You* by Joseph Christiano, ND.[3] For a brief list of fruits and vegetables suitable for each blood type and those you need to avoid, please see Appendix B.

Overview of Your Juice Fasting Program

The U.S. Department of Health and Human Services and other government organizations recommend that we eat plenty of fruits and vegetables daily, stating that we need three to five servings of vegetables and two to four servings of fruit a day to maintain health.[4] However, you may concur that few Americans eat this quantity of fruits and vegetables daily. The reason health experts recommend that our diets be based on fresh fruits and vegetables is the tremendous quantity of nutrients they contain, which our bodies desperately need for health.

Fruits and vegetables contain antioxidants, vitamins, minerals, and wonderful phytonutrients, which help to prevent cancer, heart disease, strokes, osteoporosis, and most of the other degenerative diseases. Fresh juices from vegetables and fruits are also filled with enzymes, which are organic compounds that increase the rate at which food is broken down and absorbed as fuel for the body. Cooking and processing these foods destroy these natural enzymes so necessary to our health.

Ingesting these important enzymes found in fresh vegetable and fruit juices allows your digestive system to rest from its own frenzied production of digestive enzymes so that it can repair, recuperate, and be rejuvenated. For example, the enzyme bromelain, which has been used for decades in treating inflammatory problems such as arthritis, is plentiful in pineapples. Drinking the juice made from fresh pineapples gives you extra enzyme energy, aiding digestion and numerous other clinical and therapeutic applications. Refraining from eating fats, protein, and starch also brings relief to the GI tract and other organs, such as the pancreas, which is responsible for producing digestive enzymes to break down the glut of food normally eaten.

Perhaps the most important nutrients found in vegetables and fruits are the phytonutrients, which are plant-derived nutrients containing antioxidants. These incredible nutrients can:

- Fight tumors and cancer
- Lower cholesterol
- Increase immune function
- Fight viruses
- Stimulate detoxification enzymes
- Block the production of cancer-causing compounds
- Protect DNA from damage

The pigments of the fruits and vegetables (such as the chlorophyll of green vegetables, the carotenes or carotenoids in orange fruits and vegetables, and the flavonoids in berries) contain many of these life-giving phytonutrients.[5]

Vitamins and minerals found naturally in fruits and vegetables include magnesium, folic acid, and vitamin C, which many Americans do not consume in quantities necessary for health. Green leafy vegetables are very high in magnesium and in folic acid, which are so necessary for DNA repair and to keep your immune system strong. Cooking and storage of food can easily reduce natural quantities of vitamin C. Juicing fresh fruits and vegetables assures you of getting the most nutrients from them.

Also, you need to understand the extreme value of consuming *cruciferous* vegetables, which are "cancer blasters." The word *cruciferous* comes from the same word root as *crucify*, which means to hang on a cross. The design of the flowers of cruciferous vegetables resembles elements of a cross. These important vegetables include cabbage, brussels sprouts, cauliflower, broccoli, kale, collard greens, mustard greens, turnips, and radishes. They contain more phytonutrients that have anticancer properties than any other family of vegetables.

It was God's design to place a great variety of fruits and vegetables on the earth and to give them to us for the nourishment of our bodies (Gen. 1:29). Even with the pollution of our earth today and the depletion of our soil, the quality of fresh fruits and vegetables, though diminished, still supplies wonderful, rejuvenating nutrients that will bring healing and repair to your body. And, if possible, I recommend that you locate a good source of organically grown fruits and vegetables, which will supply more nutrients and less contaminants such as pesticides.

So, if you are ready, the following chapter will outline a fasting guideline, complete with daily recipes that will help you get started. I am convinced that you will be so satisfied with the improvement in your health that juice fasting brings that you will want to make juice fasting a regular part of your fitness program.

Chapter 5

A JUICE-FASTING PROTOCOL

This chapter is designed to be your *Fasting Made Easy* guide that will give you the information you need to successfully renew your health—body, mind, and spirit—through periodic fasting. Because many people have never "denied themselves" any food item they desired at a given moment, or even considered fasting for physical or spiritual reasons, it will be important to follow these guidelines closely to learn how to begin.

I mentioned in earlier chapters the dangers and effects of a toxic body, overloaded continually with too much of the wrong kinds of food, along with the other lifestyle hazards of stress and environmental pollution. To begin to undo the damage of these health hazards too quickly could cause more problems. So, if you have never fasted or have not done so regularly, and if you think you are suffering from the effects of toxicity, please consider the following detoxification program. Remember, anyone who is suffering from disease or is under a doctor's care and taking medications needs to involve his or her physician in monitoring any fasting plan. Given those cautions, I recommend that you begin to detoxify your body by practicing the following protocols for the suggested time frame:

- Follow the liver-cleansing diet carefully for two to four weeks. (See Appendix A.)
- Take supplements recommended for a healthy liver. (See Appendix A.)
- Drink at least two quarts of filtered water daily.
- Be sure to eat plenty of fiber, especially from fresh fruits and vegetables.
- Practice periodic juice fasting for up to three days at a time (longer if monitored by a physician).
- After the juice fast, return to the liver-cleansing diet for another two weeks.

Suggested Length of Fasts

Using the guidelines I am presenting for juice fasting, I recommend that you plan to include short fasts of two to three days periodically to detoxify your body. These short fasts are effective when repeated several times a year. Repeated fasts for three days at a time are usually enough to cleanse the body. If you choose to fast for longer than three days, I recommend that you do so only under a doctor's supervision.

For my patients who have never fasted, I usually recommend that they start out by fasting one day and gradually work up to a three-day fast. With a doctor's supervision, a juice fast can be continued for one to two weeks quite safely.

Preparation for Your Juice Fast

As you begin to prepare for your juice fast, you will need to acquire the necessary items required for it.

Purchasing a juicer

First of all, you will need to purchase a juicer, a machine that makes juices out of fresh fruits and vegetables. You do not need to begin by purchasing an expensive machine; a Juice Man juicer from Wal-Mart, which costs about seventy dollars, will be sufficient. If you choose a more expensive model, such as the Champion Juicer, you will have one that will last for decades.

The Vita-Mix is a juicer that resembles a large blender and has the ability to completely juice and liquefy the entire fruit or vegetable. Of course, the added benefit for this process is the fiber you will receive in addition to the vitamins, minerals, antioxidants, enzymes, and phytonutrients present in the juice. You will need to be willing to pay several hundred dollars for this type of juicer, however. (See Appendix D.)

After you have acquired a juicer for your home, you can plan a shopping trip for lots of fresh fruits and vegetables to be consumed as juices during your fast.

Please do not substitute this step by using prepared juices in your fast. Prepared juices simply do not have the living enzymes and other vital, healing nutrients we have listed. The pasteurizing process of bottled, canned, and processed juices destroys many nutrients. This juice-fasting protocol is centered around juices from fresh fruits and vegetables prepared properly, as described.

Preparing produce

In choosing the vegetables and fruits you will use in your juice fast, I recommend that you purchase organically grown produce. They are grown without using pesticides and herbicides, which you are trying to remove from your body during the fast. Organic produce can be found in larger health food stores and, in some areas of the country, even in your supermarket.

Organic produce will usually be more expensive than regular produce and may be hard to find in some areas. If you cannot use organic produce, you will need to take special care to clean your produce before juicing in order to remove waxes and chemicals used in their production. Here are some tips for buying produce that is least affected by pesticides and herbicides and for cleansing produce that is affected:

- Look for thicker peels. Generally, the thicker the peel, the safer the fruit. For example, because of the thick peels bananas have, little pesticide usually reaches the fruit. Oranges, tangerines, lemons, grapefruits, and watermelons are also usually immune to heavy pollution from pesticides because of their thicker peel.

- Try to avoid fruits and vegetables such as apples, grapes, peaches, strawberries, kiwi, cherries, blackberries, blueberries, broccoli, lettuce, carrots, and corn, which have thin peels or none at all, if you know they have been sprayed with pesticides. Also, some fruits, such as apples, will have been waxed to seal in water and keep the fruit from spoiling for a longer time; this wax is difficult to remove.

- There are natural, biodegradable cleansers you can purchase from health food stores to wash produce that has been treated with pesticides and/or waxes. Or you may soak your produce in a mild detergent such as Ivory or pure castile soap, gently scrubbing the produce and rinsing well. Also, 1 tablespoon of a 35 percent, food-grade hydrogen peroxide (available at health food stores) may be added to a sink half-filled with water. Instead of hydrogen peroxide, you can follow the same instructions using 1 teaspoon of the Clorox bleach (not a generic brand), making sure to rinse the produce thoroughly for three to five minutes. After allowing the produce to soak for five to fifteen minutes, rinse thoroughly with fresh water.

• Remember that some fruits and vegetables contain more health benefits than others, and plan to choose those for your cleansing fast. These would include cabbage and other cruciferous vegetables, greens, dandelion root and dandelion greens, sprouts, celery, carrots, lemons and limes, apples, beets, and berries. I suggest that, for optimum detoxification, you drink one glass a day of juice that contains cruciferous vegetables such as cabbage or broccoli and beets. Also include dandelion greens or dandelion root to support the detoxification of your liver as well. (If you suffer from hypothyroidism, you may need to limit your cruciferous vegetables since they may interfere with thyroid function.)

Practical guidelines

The following practical guidelines will help you to be successful in your juice fast, especially if you have not fasted before:

• On the day before your juice fast begins, it will be very helpful to prepare your body by eating only fruits and vegetables.

• I strongly recommend that you begin your juice fast on days that you do not have to work, such as weekends. This will enable you to rest as needed in case you feel any side effects such as fatigue, lightheadedness, or headache as the body begins to do its strenuous work of detoxification.

- Refrain from drinking any beverages containing alcohol or caffeine, such as coffee or soft drinks. In addition to the fruit and vegetable juices, you may also sip soup broth made of heated vegetable juice. You can also drink herbal and green tea, along with at least two quarts of filtered water a day.

- When drinking your specially prepared juices, sip them slowly, mixing the juice with saliva. Do not gulp them down.

- I recommend that in the morning and for lunch you include juices made from fruits and vegetables. Then in the afternoon and evening, it is better to drink only vegetable juices.

- I do not recommend that you take vitamins during the fast. It would be helpful to take a number of vitamins and minerals during your two-week liver-support diet preceding your fast. (See Appendix A.) You need to stop taking all of these supplements during the actual fast period. After the fast, you should return to the liver-support diet for two additional weeks, resuming the supplementation recommended. After that, I recommend that you continue taking a comprehensive multivitamin, a comprehensive antioxidant, and a chlorophyll drink daily as part of a healthy lifestyle.

Physical Responses to Your Cleansing Fast

Your body may experience some interesting changes while fasting, so it is important to be aware of them before you begin. Not everyone will experience all of these physical responses, but in case you do, you need not be alarmed; just take necessary precautions if they occur. For example, you may experience:

- *Lightheadedness.* This is a common physical response to fasting. To avoid this uncomfortable sensation, do not stand up quickly from a lying or sitting posture. If lightheadedness does occur, lie down for a few minutes, and elevate your feet on some pillows.

- *Cold hands and feet.* It is common to experience a lowering of body temperature during a fast. The result can often be cold hands and feet. I suggest that you simply use an extra blanket at night and wear extra clothing for warmth.

- *Changes in energy.* While some people become fatigued during a fast, others actually feel more energetic. Either extreme should not alarm you. You may initially feel fatigued but gain new energy levels as your body begins to detoxify.

- *A change in sleep habits.* Your body may not require as much sleep as you are accustomed to
  requiring. Do not let this phenomenon alarm
  you. You need to plan to get plenty of rest during
  a fast, taking an afternoon siesta for about an hour
  if possible. I recommend that you limit strenuous
  exercise during the fast, taking leisurely strolls in a
  park or other slow, relaxing activities.

- *A coated tongue.* A very common symptom
  during fasting is the development of a white or
  yellow film on your tongue. This coating of the
  tongue signals a detoxification of your body.

- *Bad breath.* As toxins continue to be released
  from your body, your breath may take on an unpleasant odor. I suggest that you keep a tooth-
  brush close at hand and that you brush your teeth
  and tongue often with organic toothpaste such as
  Tom's of Maine brand.

- *A problem with constipation.* Especially during
  longer fasts, constipation can become a problem. To help prevent this problem, I recommend
  juicing pitted prunes or pitted plums along with
  apples. Also, herbal teas can help to prevent constipation, as can using a scoop of Green Superfood
  in one of the daily juices you consume.

  If you still cannot have a bowel movement, I

strongly recommend using an enema at least once a day. Simply fill an enema bag with one pint to one quart of lukewarm water. Then follow the instructions on the enema box. After insertion, it is best to first lie on your back for a minute, then on your right side, then on the stomach, and finally on your left side. Gently massaging the stomach is helpful. If problems with constipation persist, I recommend that you see a colon therapist who is able to administer colonics or colenemas. However, if you have diverticulosis, diverticulitis, Crohn's disease, or ulcerative colitis, consult your physician prior to using any kind of enema.

- *Skin eruptions.* Toxins released through fasting may result in eruptions of boils, rashes, or acne as the body detoxifies using the largest excretory organ, the skin.

- *Body odor.* As poisons exit the body through the sweat glands, some individuals will develop an offensive body odor. Warm baths help the skin and glands to slough off these toxins.

- *Darker than normal urine.* This indicates one of two things: either you are shedding large quantities of toxins through the urine, or you are not consuming adequate liquids. In either case, you need to increase your fluid intake.

- *Mucus drainage.* You may experience mucus drainage from your sinuses, bronchial tubes, or GI tract. Do not be alarmed. Again, these symptoms simply indicate that your body is using this system as well for voiding itself of many of the built-up toxins it has been storing.
- *Nausea and vomiting.* If you become mildly dehydrated, you may experience nausea and vomiting. Be sure to get enough fluids during your fast, especially the filtered water that is so important to cleansing your body.

The discomforts of the above physical responses to fasting are a small price to pay for the wonderful rewards of energy and health you will experience after cleansing your body. And the following suggestions can help aid your body in ridding itself of harmful toxins:

- *Exfoliating and cleansing the skin.* The outer, nonvascular layer of the skin covering the dermis is called the epidermis. As your body begins to detoxify during your fast, you can help keep the pores of your skin from becoming clogged by dry skin brushing. Brushing the skin daily stimulates blood and lymph flow throughout the body, helping it to remove waste more effectively.

    I recommend that you invest in a loofah

sponge or a natural soft-bristle brush. Begin by brushing the soles of your feet, and work up your legs, torso, and arms until you have brushed the majority of your body for a total of about five minutes. Avoid your face. Using firm, hard strokes, brush toward your heart to increase blood flow. Your skin will probably feel warm because you have increased circulation.

- *Infrared sauna.* An infrared sauna allows your body to secrete up to three times more perspiration and toxins than that of conventional saunas. It stimulates the cellular metabolism and breaks up the water molecules that hold toxins within the body, helping the body to excrete these toxins through perspiration.

Creativity in Combining Juices

I am including here some examples of vegetables and fruits that combine well to make healthful, tasty juices suitable for your fast. They are simply guidelines that you can use with your own creativity to develop juice combinations that are your personal favorites.

As a base for a variety of juice recipes, I recommend using a majority of the following: carrots, celery, apples, and tomatoes. One of these four choices, or a combination of them, can form the basis for an 8- to 12-ounce juice drink, which may also include smaller portions of stronger-flavored veggies, such as cabbage and greens. These stronger-flavored veggies may need to be disguised by the main four and should never make up more than one-fourth of your juice drink. Some of these stronger-flavored veggies include greens such as collard greens, spinach, broccoli, parsley, wheat grass, or dandelion greens.

You may also purchase a powdered form of vegetables, such as Green Superfood, Organic Fruit and Veggie Powder, or Living Fuel, and add a scoop to your juice drink. (See Appendix D.) They contain carefully processed nutrients of fresh vegetables in a powdered form. Organic Fruit and Veggie Powder and Berry Living Fuel also contain berries.

The following charts give juice combinations that are great for breakfast, midmorning snack, lunch, and evening portions. Again, these are only guidelines you can use to experiment with and develop your personal favorites.

Juice Combination Recipes		
Breakfast		
#1	**#2**	**#3**
½ small lemon or lime, peeled	1 pink grapefruit, peeled	Handful of parsley
1 cup berries	½ small lemon or lime, peeled	2 apples (remove seeds and core first)
3 oranges, peeled	1 apple (remove seeds and core first)	1 scoop Green Superfood (optional)
1 scoop Green Superfood (optional)	1 scoop Green Superfood (optional)	
Midmorning		
#1	**#2**	**#3**
2 celery stalks	Cut watermelon in sections, juicing enough to equal 8–12 ounces of juice (remove seeds first)	3-inch slice pineapple with skin
2 apples (remove seeds and core first)		¼ inch ginger root
2 carrots		Handful of parsley
Lunch		
#1	**#2**	**#3**
1 beet	¼–½ head of cabbage	Handful of parsley
2 carrots	Handful of collard greens	1 tomato
2 celery stalks	2 carrots	1 cucumber
½ sweet potato (uncooked)	1 apple (remove seeds and core first)	2 celery stalks
		1 garlic clove (optional)

Juice Combination Recipes		
Evening		
#1	**#2**	**#3**
4 medium toma-toes	2 carrots	4 carrots
2 celery stalks	1 beet	Handful of collard greens, spinach, or beet greens
½ cucumber	½ cucumber	1 garlic clove
Handful of alfalfa sprouts or broc-coli sprouts	2 celery stalks	Handful of parsley
1 garlic clove (op-tional)		

Vegetable juice soups

Many of the vegetable combinations are tasty when slowly warmed to be eaten as soup. However, it is important that you do not overheat them. Never boil the juices, for that will destroy their enzymes; they should be warm, not hot. Remember, you can create your own special blends. Some special vegetable juice soup recipes include the ones in the chart below.

Vegetable Juice Soups		
#1	**#2**	**#3**
2 garlic cloves	2 tomatoes	¼–½ head of cab-bage
½ cucumber	1 cucumber	2 celery stalks
2 celery stalks	2 celery stalks	2 carrots
Handful of spin-ach	1 garlic clove	Handful of parsley

Spicing it up

Adding a dash of Tabasco sauce and/or dulse powder, a tasty, salty seaweed with a reddish purple leaf, will give added flavor to your veggie juice or soups. In addition to its savory flavor, dulse is high in potassium, calcium, iron, and iodine, and it is often used for flavoring soups and salads.

Other Beverages

During your juice fast, as I have mentioned, it is very important that you drink at least 2 quarts of filtered water daily. In addition, you may want to sip various herbal teas, which are important for supporting liver detoxification, the kidneys, and the GI tract.

The blessing of herbal teas

Milk thistle and *dandelion teas* are very important in supporting the liver for detoxification. Dandelion helps to increase bile production and stimulate the gallbladder to excrete the bile, and milk thistle actually protects the liver from toxins.

Asparagus tea and *nettle tea* have diuretic properties, which help to support the kidneys that are working overtime to eliminate toxins during your fast. *Chamomile tea* has great digestive benefits as well as calming properties. I recommend that you drink chamomile tea after dinner to relax you before you retire. And *Sleepy Time Tea* has proven to be an effective herbal remedy for people who suffer from insomnia.

Smooth Move Tea can be an excellent help with bowel regularity during a juice fast. And *green tea* (decaffeinated) is very high in polyphenols called catechins. It contains two hundred times more antioxidant power than vitamin E and five hundred times more than vitamin C. I strongly recommend that you drink green tea several times a day.

Breaking Your Fast

Be prepared to discover that breaking your fast may be much more difficult than fasting itself. It is also the most important part of the fast. You will need to reintroduce foods *gradually* if you want to realize the greatest health benefits of fasting. During your fast, your digestive tract has been at rest. It has not had to produce hydrochloric acid and pancreatic enzymes needed for digestion, so they will not be readily available at the end of the fast. Dumping large quantities of whole foods into your digestive tract too soon after a fast will not only cause discomfort, but it also can actually undo some of the healing benefits of your fast.

The longer your fast time, the more time you need to take to slowly reintroduce foods into your digestive tract. If your fast is only one or two days, you can eat fruit the first day when breaking your fast. Then plan to continue eating according to the liver-support diet for two weeks as outlined in Appendix A. For a longer fast, please carefully consider the following guidelines.

Breaking a longer fast

Many who have fasted for extended periods of time concur that it is easier to fast than it is to break the fast. Breaking a fast correctly takes as much, if not more, discipline as fasting does. And it is perhaps even more important to your health than the fast itself. If you have fasted for three days or longer, you need to carefully follow these guidelines for breaking it in order to maintain the good results of the fast and to avoid introducing new problems to your digestive system:

* *First day after your fast:* You may eat fresh fruit such as grapes, watermelon, apples, or fresh berries. Every two to three hours, you may enjoy a meal of fresh fruit. I recommend that you do not eat pineapple or papaya on the first day after a fast because they contain proteolytic enzymes that could cause a stomach upset.

   Be sure to continue to drink at least two quarts of filtered water a day. And you can continue to drink the fresh juices you did during your fast.

- *Second day after your fast:* For breakfast and throughout the morning, continue with your fresh fruit regimen. For lunch and dinner you may enjoy a bowl of fresh vegetable soup. Continue your water regimen and your drinking of fresh juices during the day.

- *Third day after your fast:* Continue to eat fresh fruit in the morning and fresh vegetable soups for lunch and dinner. You may add a salad and/ or a baked potato. And you may add a slice of whole-grain bread such as brown rice or millet bread.

- *Fourth day after your fast:* To the regimens you have followed for the first three days you may add a small amount (1 or 2 ounces) of fish or free-range chicken, turkey, or lean beef. It will be very important to begin eating these proteins very slowly, chewing them well. Drink water thirty minutes before your meal, but not more than 4 ounces with your meal. It is very important that you do not yield to the temptation of overeating.

- *Fifth day on:* Gradually increase the amount of protein, and add back good fats such as nuts, seeds, and extra-virgin olive oil slowly as tolerated. Continue to add more complex carbohydrates such as beans, whole grains, and brown rice.

Again, let me emphasize the importance of properly breaking even a short fast, but especially a fast of three or more days. You simply cannot expect your digestive system to cope with normal eating patterns immediately after it has been resting for several days.

In Summary

I have included in this chapter the practical how-to guidelines to help you plan your first fast (if you have not fasted before) and to show you how to maintain a lifestyle that includes regular fasting, which will ensure health in the long term. The physical benefits of fasting cannot be overestimated, whether you simply feel sluggish and need more energy, or if you are suffering from illness or disease. Giving the body a chance to demonstrate its ability to heal when given the proper nourishment for cleansing can bring a dramatic change to your energy levels and overall health.

Chapter 6

A FASTED LIFESTYLE

If you are among those who think they can correct their health problems by "gutting out" a three-day fast and then returning to their typical high-sugar, high-processed starches, high-fat, and red meat diet, let me caution you concerning that erroneous thinking. Returning to a lifestyle that caused your body to become toxic in the first place, often resulting in degenerative disease, will only continue the cycle of poor health.

Consider a person who stops smoking for a month and then goes back to a two-pack-a-day cigarette habit. The good he or she accomplished in that month of not smoking will soon be undone because of returning to the old unhealthy habit. Only if you allow your detoxification program and fast to be the beginning of a new, healthier lifestyle will you truly reap the benefits of it.

Healthy Eating

I suggest that, in order to make the detoxification process an ongoing lifestyle, you make it a habit to drink 8 to 16 ounces of juiced vegetables and fruits daily. Also, continue using the Green Superfood, Organic Fruit and Veggie Powder, or Living Fuel on a daily basis, as they represent about five to six servings of vegetables.

It will also be important to continue to eat plenty of fruits, vegetables, and whole grains as well as legumes, nuts, and seeds. You may safely eat smaller amounts of lean, free-range meats and poultry. I recommend that you limit or avoid dairy, choosing skim milk products if you continue to consume dairy. And it is important to avoid processed foods, hydrogenated and partially hydrogenated fats, and fried foods, choosing instead good fats such as extra-virgin olive oil. Limit the amounts of saturated fats such as organic butter. Continue to experiment with any vegetables and fruit that are compatible with your blood type, allowing your body to be more effectively nourished by them.

Know your categories

Include the following foods in your daily diet, and you will have less inclination to eat harmful foods:

- Freshly squeezed juices
- Water—consume plenty of filtered or bottled water
- Nuts (especially almonds, walnuts, and Macadamia nuts) and seeds (such as pumpkinseeds, sunflower seeds, sesame seeds, or flaxseed)
- Whole-grain breads such as Ezekiel, rye, spelt, millet, or brown rice bread

- Leafy greens for salads
- Fresh organic fruits and vegetables
- Organically farmed eggs, known as choice eggs
- Free-range or organically raised chicken
- Fish such as salmon, mackerel, halibut, and flounder
- Rice, almond, soy, and sesame milk
- Fresh herbs and herbal teas

Avoid the junk

Eating the above foods in abundance will help you to forgo the temptation to eat the following harmful foods that should be limited or avoided:

- Sugar
- Wheat pasta
- Coffee, black tea, and other caffeinated beverages
- Dairy products (milk, cheese, yogurt, cream)
- Alcohol
- Salt
- White rice
- Fried foods
- Carbonated beverages
- Corn
- Artificial sweeteners like aspartame
- Hydrogenated and partially hydrogenated fats
- Processed foods such as white bread, bagels, crackers, and pretzels

• Artificial food additives and artificially colored foods

Don't expect to eat completely healthy all at once, especially if you have developed poor eating habits for years. But try to eliminate a few of these harmful foods for a season.

Fasting helps to break food addictions and other unhealthy eating habits. After a fast, fresh fruits and vegetables taste wonderful. And you won't desire to "binge" or overeat as you receive the nourishment your body needs. Periodic fasting can do wonders to help you adopt healthy eating as a lifestyle.

Healthy Exercise

I recommend that to ensure a healthy, fasted lifestyle, you plan to include a good exercise program. Many toxins can be expelled simply through perspiration as you give your body the exercise it needs. Exercise is also an antidote for stress, helping to relax tight muscles and release the tension of the day.

Aerobic exercise helps to calm your body as well as your mind by releasing tension. Regular aerobic exercise does not need to be dreaded; it can be a lot of fun. You may want to get together with friends for a walk, tennis, or a bike ride instead of meeting "over lunch." You could consider joining a square dancing club or taking ballroom dancing lessons. Choose to exercise in a way that is enjoyable for you, and you will more likely succeed in it.

The benefits of regular exercise include improved heart health, lung function, circulation, and blood pressure. Exercise can actually decrease fatigue as it relaxes your muscles and reduces stress. As you exercise, your body also releases endorphins, which are natural antidepressants and pain relievers, which results in your feeling better after you exercise.

If you want an easy, natural way to boost your self-image, build your confidence, and increase your energy, determine to exercise at least twenty minutes a day, three days a week.

Simple relaxation

Sometimes it is the simple discovery of slowing down to enjoy quietness that becomes an important form of exercise. Our society's stress level is often induced by the continual noises that greet us from the time we get up in the morning—TV or radio blaring as we prepare for work, rush hour traffic muffled by the car stereo, and voices and other sounds throughout the day. Releasing some of the stress that results from daily routines can be effectively accomplished by quiet, relaxation techniques.

Why not try the following deep-breathing exercises to release some built-up tension and stress?[1]

- Find a quiet place, and sit or lie down in a comfortable position. Close your eyes, and place one hand on your chest and the other hand on your abdomen. Determine where your breathing is coming from. Is it coming from your chest or abdomen? Abdominal breathing has a calming effect on the body. However, most people are chest breathers.

- Correct your shallow, stress-filled breathing by lying on your back. Place a book on your lower abdomen below your navel. As you breathe in, the book should rise. As you breathe out, it should sink.

- Breathe in deeply and slowly. Pause and relax.

- Repeat until you begin to feel calmer and more relaxed.

The following progressive muscle relaxation exercise can relax your entire body in about twenty minutes:[2]

1. Sit or lie down quietly in a comfortable position away from noise or distractions.

2. Tense and tighten your muscles in each of the following muscle groups, beginning at your head. Tense each body part for five seconds, then slowly release the tension as you focus on the body part. Repeat this twice for each muscle group:

- Forehead and top of head—raise eyebrows
- Jaw—clench teeth
- Neck—pull chin forward onto your chest, then push your head back slowly
- Shoulders and trapezius muscles—lift shoulders
- Back—pull back shoulder blades
- Arms—flex biceps
- Abdomen —tighten abdomen
- Buttocks—squeeze and tighten buttocks
- Thighs—flex thighs
- Calves—flex and point toes up or down

As you learn to slowly release the tension in your muscles through this exercise, you will actually be teaching your body how to relax. Your mind and body crave the wonderful release that regular patterns of healthy exercise give them.

Healthy Choices

It is important that you continue to make healthy choices regarding every area of your lifestyle. To enhance your fasted lifestyle, I recommend that you establish a regular cleansing process to help your body maintain health before you experience symptoms of toxin-induced illness.

Periodic cleansing: "master cleanse"

One of the best ways to help maintain your body's detoxification is to fast periodically with special fasting recipes. The Master Cleanse is an excellent recipe for fasting:[3]

2 Tbsp. fresh squeezed lemon or lime juice

1 Tbsp. 100 percent pure maple syrup (from a health food store)

$\frac{1}{10}$ tsp. cayenne pepper

8 oz. spring water

Liquid Stevia to taste (natural sweetener)

If you are going to consume this cleansing liquid for one day, mix and drink eight to twelve glasses during the day. Do not eat or drink anything else except water or the herbal teas mentioned previously. A periodic "master cleanse" (once a week, once a month, or a two- to three-day fast every few months) helps your body's natural ability to detoxify, keeping it from getting overloaded with environmental as well as dietary toxins.

Living Fuel (or Berry Living Fuel)

A wonderful product, which I mentioned earlier, for maintaining the cleansing process is called *Living Fuel*. It consists of juiced vegetables in powdered form and is an excellent alternative for those individuals with too little time for juicing. A companion product, *Berry Living Fuel*, is also available, which contains berries. I recommend two scoops three times a day of either product during a fast with an additional 2 quarts of filtered water. For maintenance after the fast, I recommend only two scoops a day. (See Appendix D for more information.)

Living Fuel provides an excellent method for fasting that Type 2 diabetics can use. (If you are a Type 1 diabetic, you should not fast. Type 2 diabetics should only fast under the supervision of a physician.) It is designed to detoxify the body and repair a damaged metabolism by removing the stress caused from eating everyday foods. It provides everything the body needs to thrive in a restricted caloric format for a short time.

While I have addressed comprehensively the wonderful benefits of cleansing the body through fasting and the physical benefits of living a fasted lifestyle, I do not want to neglect the spiritual dimension of fasting and the benefits it can bring to us. The benefits of fasting do not end with improved physical health. There are wonderful spiritual benefits received from fasting as well, benefits that can improve your mental and spiritual health and help you discover your life destiny.

Conclusion

As we have explored the ancient ritual of fasting, given a position of honor since biblical times, I hope you have concluded that fasting is a powerful tool for health, cleansing, and spiritual empowerment.

I recommend that you choose to fast periodically for detoxification purposes and that you commit your fasting time to God for spiritual cleansing and renewal as well. Fasting is a biblical key to health that will bring renewed vitality, healing, longevity, and deeper spirituality to your life. I consider fasting to be a privilege, and I encourage you to learn to devote increasing portions of your fasting time to Bible reading, prayer, studying spiritual growth books such as *The Purpose Driven Life*, and journaling for personal and spiritual growth.

I truly believe that fasting with the right motivation will lead you in the footsteps of great men and women who have lived before us and who, through fasting, touched heaven with their prayers and nations with their passion, increasing personally in purity of body, mind, and spirit. I commend you for choosing to read *Fasting Made Easy*, and I encourage you to take ownership of this powerful tool.

Epilogue

After reading this book, hopefully you feel motivated to cleanse and detoxify your body on a regular basis. You may be suffering from severe fatigue and exhaustion, and chronic pain, or perhaps you have been stricken with a chronic disease such as rheumatoid arthritis, lupus, or psoriasis. Realize that there is hope, but *you* must begin to choose living foods in place of the dead foods so typical to the American diet.

God declared to His people, "I have set before you life and death, the blessing and the curse. So choose life in order that you may live, you and your descendants" (Deut. 30:19). He is declaring that to you as well. You must begin to choose life by choosing living foods over dead foods so that your body can begin to heal. Remember, if you keep doing the same thing you have always done, you will most likely continue to suffer from the same health problems.

As Christians, our lives are to be filled with the fruit of the Spirit: love, joy, peace, patience, kindness, goodness, faithfulness, gentleness, and self-control (Gal. 5:22–23). Too many people are neglecting the developing of self-control in their eating habits.

Begin to practice self-control by simply choosing foods that bring life instead of foods that bring death.

Periodic fasting enables you to develop the fruit of self-control in your life. Allow juice fasting to cleanse your body on a cellular level, and watch as your health begins to spring forth speedily.

NUTRITIONAL PROGRAM
DESIGNED FOR YOUR LIVER

Before you consider fasting, it is important to follow this uniquely designed nutritional program to strengthen and support your liver, which will prepare it for the increased role of detoxification during your fast. You need to follow this diet and regimen of supplements for a period of two weeks to prepare your body for fasting as well as to restore your body following the fast.

These dietary guidelines will help cleanse and support your liver before and after your detox fast. The more closely you follow these guidelines, the more benefit you will receive from your fast. It is important that you change your diet and lifestyle to reduce the amount of toxins you are taking in as well as improve your body's ability to eliminate toxins.

Eliminate Toxins

Avoid cigarette smoke, alcohol, and drugs. Decrease your intake of all medications. Of course, for prescription medicines, you must do this with your doctor's help. Be sensible; never make drastic changes without consulting your doctor.

Foods to Avoid

Making the right choices of food for your liver's health is important, especially before you consider detoxification through fasting. Here are some foods (and other products) to avoid:

- Coffee, colas, and chocolate
- Alcohol
- Processed vegetable oils
- Animal skins
- Fatty meats
- Preserved meats
- Deep-fried foods
- Hydrogenated and partially hydrogenated fats (margarine)
- Refined foods
- Simple sugars, including honey
- Fast foods
- Dark teas (green tea is OK)

  Decrease your consumption of the following:

- Meat (choose extra-lean, free-range meats and poultry)
- Dairy products (choose skim milk, plain yogurt or kefir, and small amounts of organic butter if you must have dairy products)
- Saturated fats—cheese, marbled meats (choose skim milk cheese or soy cheese and lean meats)

Foods to Eat

For at least two weeks, in preparation for your fast, eat as many of the following foods as possible:

- Organic fruit: Drink a glass of freshly juiced fruits and vegetables in the morning instead of coffee.
- Organic vegetables: Eat as many raw vegetables as possible. In addition, the cruciferous vegetables, such as cabbage, cauliflower, brussels sprouts, broccoli, kale, collard greens, mustard greens, and turnips, are essential. Other liver-friendly vegetables include legumes (all types of beans), beets, carrots, dandelion root, and greens.
- Liver-friendly starches: Eat brown rice, wild rice, rice pasta, and brown rice bread. (Avoid wheat products, including breads, bagels, crackers, pasta, chips, and cereals, as well as corn products.)
- Good fats for your liver and for detoxification: Use extra-virgin olive oil; avocados; raw, fresh nuts and seeds (avoid peanuts and cashews); flaxseed oil (not for cooking); evening primrose oil; black currant seed oil; borage oil; and fish oil.
- Important proteins: Eat portions of 4 to 6 ounces of salmon, mackerel, herring, or halibut; eat 2 to 4 ounces of free-range, extra-lean chicken and turkey.
- Beverages: Drink plenty of filtered water with

fresh-squeezed lemon or lime (two quarts daily), fresh vegetable and fruit juices, green tea, and other herbal teas.

Supplements for the Liver

There are certain supplements that are very important to the liver, which you should take to prepare for a detoxification fast and when ending a fast. For a complete discussion of important liver supplements, please see my book *Toxic Relief.* Following is a summary of these important supplements:

- A comprehensive multivitamin and mineral supplement daily (such as Divine Health Multivitamins)
- A comprehensive antioxidant formula (such as Divine Health Elite Antioxidant)
- Milk thistle
- Amino acids (NAC is the most important)
- Detox teas, dandelion tea

Appendix D contains information for ordering these supplements.

JUICE FASTING ACCORDING TO BLOOD TYPE

The following lists contain basic choices of fruits and vegetables that are beneficial for each blood type, those that are neutral (neither harmful nor extremely beneficial), and those that should be avoided by people with that blood type.

Blood Type A

Highly beneficial

VEGETABLES: Artichokes, beet leaves, broccoli, carrots, chicory, collard greens, dandelion, escarole, garlic, horseradish, kale, kohlrabi, leek, lettuce, romaine, okra, onions (red, Spanish, yellow), parsley, parsnips, pumpkin, spinach, sprouts (alfalfa), Swiss chard, tempeh, tofu, turnips

FRUITS: Apricots, blackberries, blueberries, cherries, cranberries, figs, grapefruit, lemons, pineapple, plums, prunes, raisins

Neutral

VEGETABLES: Arugula, asparagus, avocado, bamboo shoots, beets, bok choy, caraway, cauliflower, celery, chervil, coriander, corn, cucumber, daikon radish, dill, endive, fennel, fiddlehead ferns, ginger, lettuces, mushrooms (enoki, portobello, oyster), mustard greens, olives (green), onions (green), radicchio, radishes, rappini, rutabaga, scallions/shallots, seaweed, sprouts (brussels, mung, radish), squash (all types), water chestnut, watercress, zucchini

FRUITS: Apples, currants, dates, elderberries, grapes (all kinds), guava, kiwi, kumquat, limes, loganberries, melon (canang, casaba, Christmas, Crenshaw, musk, Spanish, watermelon), nectarine, peaches, pears, persimmons, pomegranates, prickly pear, starfruit, strawberries

Avoid

VEGETABLES: Cabbage (Chinese, red, white), eggplant, lima beans, mushrooms (domestic, shiitake), mustard greens, olives (black, Greek, Spanish), peppers (green, jalapeno, red, yellow), potatoes (sweet, red, white), tomatoes, yams

FRUITS: Bananas, coconuts, mangoes, melon (cantaloupe, honeydew), oranges, papayas, plantains, rhubarb, tangerines[1]

Blood Type B

Highly beneficial

VEGETABLES: Beets, beet leaves, broccoli, cabbage (Chinese, red, white), carrots, cauliflower, collard greens, eggplant, kale, lima beans, mushrooms (shiitake), mustard greens, parsley, parsnips, peppers (green, red, jalapeno, red, yellow), potatoes (sweet), sprouts (brussels), yams

FRUITS: Bananas, cranberries, grapes (black, concord, green, red), papaya, pineapple, plums

Neutral

VEGETABLES: Arugula, asparagus, avocado, bamboo shoots, bok choy, celery, chervil, chicory, cucumber, daikon radish, dandelion, dill, endive, escarole, fennel, fiddlehead ferns, garlic, ginger, horseradish, kohlrabi, leek, lettuce (all types), mushrooms (domestic, enoki, portobello, tree oyster), okra, onions (green, red, Spanish, yellow), radicchio, rappini, rutabaga, scallions, seaweed, shallots, snow peas, spinach, sprouts (alfalfa), Swiss chard, turnips, water chestnuts, watercress, zucchini

FRUITS: Apples, apricots, blackberries, blueberries, boysenberries, cherries, currants, dates, elderberries, figs, gooseberries, grapefruit, guava, kiwi, kumquat, lemons, limes, loganberries, melon (all types), nectarines, oranges, peaches, raisins, pears, prunes, plantains, strawberries, tangerines

Avoid

VEGETABLES: Artichokes (domestic and Jerusalem), avocado, corn (yellow, white), olives (black, green, Greek, Spanish), pumpkin, radishes, sprouts (mung, radish), tempeh, tofu, tomato

FRUITS: Coconuts, persimmons, pomegranates, prickly pear, rhubarb, starfruit[2]

Blood Type AB

Highly beneficial

VEGETABLES: Beet leaves, beets, broccoli, cauliflower, celery, collard greens, cucumber, dandelion, garlic, kale, mustard greens, eggplant, parsley, parsnips, potatoes (sweet), sprouts (alfalfa), tempeh, tofu, yams

FRUITS: Cherries, cranberries, figs, grapes, kiwi, loganberries, gooseberries, grapefruit, lemons, pineapple, plums, prunes

Neutral

VEGETABLES: Arugula, asparagus, bamboo shoots, horseradish, bok choy, cabbage (red, Chinese, white), caraway, carrots, chervil, coriander, daikon radish, dill, endive, escarole, fennel, fiddlehead ferns, tomato, ginger, lettuce, leeks, mushrooms, potatoes (red, white), okra, pumpkin, olives (green, Spanish), onions (all), radicchio, rappini, rutabaga, shallots, scallions, snow peas, seaweed, sprouts (brussels, mung, radish), squash (all types), water chestnut, watercress, zucchini

FRUITS: Apples, apricots, berries (black, blue), boysenberries, currants, dates, elderberries, kumquats, limes, papayas, tangerines, melon (cantaloupe, casaba, Christmas, Crenshaw, musk, Spanish, watermelons), nectarine, peaches, pears, plantains, prunes, raisins, raspberries, strawberries

Avoid

VEGETABLES: Artichokes, corn, avocado, lima beans, mushrooms (shiitake), olives (black), peppers (green, jalapeno, red, yellow), sprouts (mung, radish)

FRUITS: Bananas, coconuts, guava, mangoes, oranges, persimmons, pomegranates, prickly pears, rhubarb, starfruit[3]

Blood Type O

Highly beneficial

VEGETABLES: Artichokes, beet leaves, broccoli, chicory, collard greens, dandelion, escarole, garlic, horseradish, kale, kohlrabi, leek, lettuce (romaine), okra, onions (red, Spanish, yellow), parsley, parsnips, peppers (red), potatoes (sweet), pumpkin, seaweed, spinach, Swiss chard, turnips

FRUITS: Figs, plums, prunes

Neutral

VEGETABLES: Arugula, asparagus, bamboo shoots, beets, bok choy, caraway, celery, carrots, chervil, coriander, cucumbers, daikon, dill, endive, fennel, fiddlehead ferns, ginger, lettuce, lima beans, mushrooms (enoki, portobello, oyster), olives (green), onions (green), peppers (green, yellow, jalapeno), radicchio, radishes, rappini, rutabaga, scallions, shallots, snow peas, sprouts (mung, radish), squash (all types), tempeh, tofu, tomato, water chestnut, watercress, yams, zucchini

FRUITS: Apples, apricots, bananas, blueberries, boysenberries, cherries, cranberries, currants, dates, elderberries, gooseberries, grapefruit, grapes, guava, kiwi, kumquat, lemons, limes, mangoes, melons (casaba, Crenshaw, musk, watermelon), nectarines, papayas, peaches, pears, persimmons, pineapples, pomegranates, prickly pear, raisins, raspberries, starfruit

Avoid

VEGETABLES: Avocado, cabbage (Chinese, red, white), cauliflower, corn (white, yellow), eggplant, mushroom (domestic, shiitake), mustard greens, olives (black, Greek, Spanish), potatoes (red, white), sprouts (alfalfa, brussels)

FRUITS: Blackberries, coconuts, melon (cantaloupe, honeydew), oranges, plantains, rhubarb, strawberries, tangerines[4]

Appendix C

YOUR FASTING JOURNAL

Maintaining a simple journal during your fast will help you to grow and develop as a total person—body, mind, and spirit. During your fast, it is important that you set aside time for reflecting, journaling, prayer, and Bible reading.

Dedicating a special notebook to your fasting journal, include a place for each day's prayers, prayer requests, thoughts, and insights. List particular reasons for your fast, including physical, mental, and spiritual aspects.

You will want to include also any foods (juices) you consumed on a given day to which you think you may be having a reaction, choosing to eliminate them to confirm any food allergies you may be experiencing.

As you make periodic fasting a part of your life, continue to make new entries in your journal, noting spiritual "breakthroughs" as well as physical and mental benefits you have experienced.

Prayer Suggestions

Make prayer a priority during your fast, setting aside

certain specific times for prayer and journaling. And follow these suggestions for your spiritual fast:

- Listen quietly to hear the voice of the Holy Spirit.
- Write in your journal the impressions you receive from the Holy Spirit.
- Record your prayer requests, and date them when you receive an answer.
- As you read the Bible, record special insights and encouragement you receive from certain passages.
- Be sure to record praise reports of benefits received from the fast.
- If you have any significant dreams during your fast, record them and pray for a spiritual interpretation.

It is important during your fast that you be expecting God to do wonderful things in your life as you obey Christ's instructions to follow Him in fasting. You can expect answers to prayer as well as bondages in your life to be broken, along with the natural healing fasting offers the body. Your testimony will help to inspire others to overcome the flesh through periodic fasting, bringing the favor of God on their lives as well.

Appendix D

RESOURCES

For your convenience, I have listed contact information for the following products, which I discussed in this book:

UltraGlycemX and UltraClear Plus by Metagenics

Call Metagenics at 1-800-647-6100. Use Dr. Colbert's ID number COL1210-93 when calling.

Living Fuel (regular or berry flavor)

Call 1-813-254-5150 or their toll-free number 1-866-580-FUEL (3835) to order. You can also visit their Web site at www.divinelivingfuel.com.

Digestive stool analysis with parasitology, intestinal permeability testing, and food allergy testing

Contact Great Smokies Diagnostic Laboratories at their Web site, www.gsdl.com.

Blood-type diet

Peter J. D'Adamo, ND, *Eat Right for Your Type* (New York: Putnam's Sons, 1997).

Joseph Christiano, ND, *Bloodtypes, Bodytypes and You* (Lake Mary, FL: Siloam, 2000, 2004).

Divine Health products

To order Green Superfood, Divine Health Organic

Fruit and Veggie Powder, Divine Health Whole Food Multivitamin, Divine Health Buffered Vitamin C, Divine Health Elite Antioxidant, and other Divine Health products, call 1-407-331-7007 or visit the Web site at www.drcolbert.com.

Vita-Mix Mixer

Visit their Web site at www.Vita-Mix.com.

Wellness water and shower filters

Call Wellness Filters at 1-888-611-0112.

Infrared sauna

Contact QCA Spas and/or TheraSauna at 1-563-359-3881. Or you can visit their Web site at www.qcaspas.com or e-mail them at qcaspas@qcaspas.com.

The Alkalizer Water System

For more information, e-mail info@alkalizer.com. DBS, Inc. is offering Dr. Colbert's readers a $100 discount on the unit. Simply supply this code when ordering: DC7007.

To locate a nutritional doctor

Call ACAM at 1-800-LEAD-OUT (1-800-532-3688).

Notes

Chapter 1 — Why Should I Fast?

1. J. Beasley, et al., "The Kellogg Report: The Impact of Nutrition, Environment and Lifestyle on the Health of Americans," New York Institute of Health Policy and Practice, The Baird College Center, 1989.

2. Stephen Edelsen, *What Your Doctor May Not Tell You About Autoimmune Disorders* (New York: Warner Books, Inc., 2003).

3. Don Colbert, MD, *Toxic Relief* (Lake Mary, FL: Siloam, 2001, 2003), 210–211.

4. "Sugar Consumption 'Off The Charts' Say Health Experts: HHS/USDA Urged to Commission Review of Sugar's Health Impact," Center for Science in the Public Interest News Release, December 30, 1998, http://www.cspinet.org/new/sugar.html (accessed March 17, 2004).

5. Ibid.

6. Ibid.

Chapter 2 — Physical Benefits of Fasting

1. Arnold Ehret, *Mucusless Diet and Healing System* (Beaumont, CA: Ehret Literature, 1972).

2. Dean Ornish, et al., "Can Lifestyle Changes Reverse Coronary Heart Disease?" *Lancet* 336 (1990): 129–133.

Chapter 3 — Mental and Spiritual Benefits of Fasting

1. J. B. Lightfoot, *The Apostolic Fathers,* edited and completed by J. R. Harner (Grand Rapids, MI: Baker Books Press, 1956).

Chapter 4 — How Should I Fast?

1. Daniel 1:8–16, from *Matthew Henry's Commentary on the Whole Bible: New Modern Edition*, Electronic Database. Copyright (c) 1991 by Hendrickson Publishers, Inc.

2. Ibid.

3. Peter J. D'Adamo, ND, *Eat Right for Your Type* (New York: Putnam's Sons, 1997). Joseph Christiano, ND, *Bloodtypes, Bodytypes and You* (Lake Mary, FL: Siloam, 2000, 2004).

4. AMS at USDA, Fruit and Vegetable Programs, Agricultural Marketing Service @ USDA, http://www.ams.usda.gov/fv/ (accessed March 24, 2004).

5. For a more detailed discussion of phytonutrients, please refer to my book *Toxic Relief*, 64–72.

Chapter 6 — A Fasted Lifestyle

1. Don Colbert, MD, *The Bible Cure for Irritable Bowel Syndrome* (Lake Mary, FL: Siloam, 2002), 58–59.

2. Ibid., 60–61

3. Elson M. Haas, MD, *Staying Healthy With Nutrition* (Berkeley, CA: Celestial Arts Pub., 1992).

Appendix B — Juice Fasting According to Blood Type

1. D'Adamo, *Eat Right for Your Type*, 334.

2. Ibid., 335.

3. Ibid., 336.

4. Ibid., 333.

Strang Communications, the publisher of both Charisma House and *Charisma* magazine, wants to give you a FREE SUBSCRIPTION to our award-winning magazine.

Since its inception in 1975, *Charisma* magazine has helped thousands of Christians stay connected with what God is doing worldwide.

Within its pages you will discover in-depth reports and the latest news from a Christian perspective, biblical health tips, global events in the body of Christ, personality profiles, and so much more. Join the family of *Charisma* readers who enjoy feeding their spirit each month with miracle-filled testimonies and inspiring articles that bring clarity, provoke prayer, and demand answers.

To claim your **3 free issues** of *Charisma,* send your name and address to: Charisma 3 Free Issue Offer, 600 Rinehart Road, Lake Mary, FL 32746. Or you may call 1-800-829-3346 and ask for Offer # 93FREE. This offer is only valid in the USA.

---

www.charismamag.com